THE ABSENT FATHER

APOSTLE LUDLOW HAYNES

THE ABSENT FATHER

Copyright ©2024 Apostle Ludlow Haynes

Paperback ISBN: 978-1-957809-84-7

All rights reserved. No part of this publication may be reproduced, distributed, or transmitted in any form or by any means, including photocopying, recording, or other electronic or mechanical methods without the prior written permission of the author except in the case of brief quotations embodied in reviews and certain other non-commercial uses permitted by copyright law.

Published by Cornerstone Publishing

A Division of Cornerstone Creativity Group LLC
Info@thecornerstonepublishers.com
www.thecornerstonepublishers.com

Author's Contact

To book the author to speak at your next event or to order bulk copies of this book, please, use the information below:

Apostlehaynes50@gmail.com

Printed in the United States of America.

DEDICATION

To my wife, Pastor Cecile Haynes, and my daughter, Co-Pastor Tracy-Ann Morgan.

Contents

DEDICATION III

Introduction:
The Absent Father 1

Chapter One
Fatherhood Is Everything 5

Chapter Two
The Trauma of an Absent Father 19

Chapter Three
Why Fathers Leave 33

Chapter Four
The Struggles of Single Mothers 47

Chapter Five
Healing from Absent Father's Wound 61

Chapter Six
Breaking the Curse of Absentee Fathers 77

Chapter Seven
Strategies for Reconnection 89

Chapter Eight
A Final Word for Everyone 103

REFERENCES 113

ABOUT THE BOOK 115

Introduction:
THE ABSENT FATHER

Fatherhood is a sacred bond ordained by God to provide spiritual covering, emotional support, physical protection, and financial provision for children. Unfortunately, we live in a fallen and broken world with irregularities. Fathers abandon their families, while women are subject to untold responsibilities, and this makes the whole family completely devastated.

There is a growing crisis of absent fathers, which deprives many children of paternal love and support. Statistics reveal that over 18 million children in the United States live without their biological father in the home.

What could be responsible for this ugly trend? Why would any father want to leave their wife and children behind? In many cases, a father's absence may result from a divorce. However, not all fathers' absence is caused by divorce; in some cases, separation can result from other factors such as incarceration, migrations for work, or war. A wrong attitude from the wife can also drive a father away.

On the other hand, a father might not be physically absent but emotionally separated from the children. For instance, despite being physically present, a father who is a workaholic or an alcoholic can still be emotionally detached from his children.

Either way, a father's absence has a far-reaching adverse effect on children, mothers, fathers, and society. Sometimes, what causes fathers to leave home is beyond their control, yet the impacts can last a lifetime.

The Absent Father explores the impact of absentee fatherhood on children's emotional, psychological, behavioral, social, and physical well-being. It also gives voice to the struggles of single mothers left with an overwhelming burden, examines the guilt and regret fathers often feel, and highlights the vicious cycle that frequently perpetuates across generations. It also delivers a robust template for strengthening weak and broken families.

Most importantly, "The Absent Father" stresses the importance of reconnection between fathers and their children. Through focused case studies, personal narratives, and research, we outlined strategies for fathers to overcome barriers and rebuild trust, coupled with the legal framework for initiating a reconnection.

By discovering why many fathers leave and the key factors that drive absentee fatherhood, we position ourselves to eliminate the menace of absent fatherhood. The insights shared in this book prove valuable in shaping perspectives and enabling connections between all parties involved. The book concludes with counsel for everyone caught in the absentee father web.

Whether you are a single mother carrying the burden of an entire family by yourself, an abandoned child suffering from emotional wounds, or a father waking up to the impact of your absence, this book will transform your life!

Chapter One
FATHERHOOD IS EVERYTHING

There is no greater gift than the gift of a father's presence in the lives of his children. It is fascinating for a child to know that his father will be available whenever he calls. We cannot overemphasize the role of a father to his children. The greatest thing a father can do for his family is to be available.

The father's presence tremendously impacts the children's upbringing, development, and wellbeing. From providing emotional and financial support to shaping values and providing guidance and security, fathers play vital roles in their children's lives. Committed and loving fathers can make all the difference in helping children reach their full potential.

Unfortunately, many children grow up without an actively involved father figure. Surprisingly, this seems to be a growing trend today. According to the U.S. Census Bureau, about 1 in 4 children under the age of 18 live without the presence of their biological father in the home. That figure equates to nearly 17 million minors. And it goes even as high as 50% in the African American community compared to 20% for white children. According to data provided by NCHS, about 25% of kids also have no contact at all with their biological fathers, per Census stats.

Such alarming statistics point to the crisis surrounding the father's absence and its overwhelming consequences, not just for the children but for society at large. The adverse effects of this absence have been found to have a more far-reaching impact on children than any of us can imagine.

However, despite the growing trend of absentee fathers, many continue to exert tremendous positive influence on their children. And the reason is because they have found a way to be present in their children's lives. Moreover, they seem to understand the critical nature of their role in their children's lives.

This chapter will focus on understanding who a father is, the critical roles that fathers play in their children's lives, and the power of a father's presence in the home. Does fatherhood truly matter? One may ask. Of course, it does. Fatherhood is everything.

UNDERSTANDING FATHERHOOD

Who is a father? Firstly, the word fathers is from the Hebrew word âb (pronounced as awb) and the Greek word patēr, which means originator or male ancestor, progenitor of a people. Father connotes an individual's father, head of, or founder of a household, group, family, or clan. It also means originator or producer.

Fatherhood goes far beyond biological ties or genetic makeup. A father nurtures, guides, provides for, and shapes a young child's life with love and wisdom. And men are the scripturally ordained object of fatherhood. Part of how men demonstrate fatherhood daily is by how they show care and compassion towards children in their family, sphere, and community.

There are two main types of fathers: Biological fathers and spiritual fathers. Your biological father is someone by whose seed you came into the earthly realm. He is the one who is responsible for your being, naturally speaking. But then, there is spiritual fatherhood. Your spiritual father describes someone who led you to Christ—someone by whom you received the gospel and gave your heart to the Lord.

Spiritual fathers are often Clergymen and mentors who offer spiritual guidance, mental nurturing, and emotional support just like a biological father. To be a spiritual father requires maturity, ethics, and wisdom to positively influence young people in the way of God and success.

In another sense, a spiritual father is someone by whom you are being groomed spiritually. A good example is Eli and Samuel. Samuel was a spiritual son of Eli (1 Sam 3:1 - 10). Samuel was groomed into his calling by Eli. A spiritual father plays a critical role in the lives of their spiritual sons and daughters. A spiritual father infuses his spirit into his spiritual children. That is called impartation (Deuteronomy 34:9). In this book, we shall focus on biological fathers.

A biological father is the man from whose loins a child is conceived. Of course, we know that children originate from their parents, particularly their fathers. The seed of the man planted into the mother's womb produces the child. The body of the child comes from the mother, but the originating seed proceeds from the father's loins. In other words, where there are no fathers, there are no children. Fatherhood is God's divine order for procreation and replicating his purposes on earth.

Aside from being the originator and progenitor of something, a father is a transmitter of ideas. Since a father is the originator of not just children but also ideas, concepts, and products, then fatherhood is attributable to corporate non-biological entities like an organization. A person who founded an organization, business, or idea can be referred to as the father of such concept, idea, product, or business.

SOURCE AND SUSTAINER.

Another compelling concept of a father is that of source and sustainer. Whatever the source of anything is, it is usually the sustainer of it. In other words, if you originate from a particular source, you must constantly remain connected to and depend on that source for sustenance.

FROM THE LENS OF OUR HEAVENLY FATHER

To fully appreciate the place and role of our earthly fathers, we need to understand the place of our Heavenly Father. One of the Bible's first and most prominent teachings is that God is a creator (Genesis chapters 1 and 2). But God is not just a creator but also a loving Father. God is the creator of all creation but a loving and caring father to all who believe in Him. Through faith in Christ, we are adopted as the father's sons and daughters (Romans 8:14-17). Of course, there are several aspects to God's fatherhood from Scripture: As a father, God Almighty plays several roles in the lives of His children.

GOD IS A PROVIDER

Just as an earthly father provides for the needs of his children, God provides for His children. The Scripture promises that God will supply all his children's needs according to his riches in glory (Philippians 4:19). In Matthew's gospel, we are admonished to not worry about what we would eat, drink, or clothes to put on, seeing that our Heavenly Father knows and cares for us so much that He made these provisions available for us. We are told that He feeds the birds of the air and clothes the lilies of the field. And if He cares for these little creatures, how much more his very own children. He would do even much more for His children.

"Therefore I say unto you, Take no thought for your life, what ye shall eat, or what ye shall drink; nor yet for your body, what ye shall put on. Is not life more than meat, and is the body more than raiment?

Behold the fowls of the air: for they sow not, neither do they reap, nor gather into barns; yet your heavenly father feedeth them. Are ye not much better than they? By taking thought, which of you can add one cubit unto his stature?

And why take ye thought for raiment? Consider the lilies of the field, how they grow; they toil not, neither do they spin: And yet I say unto you, That even Solomon in all his glory was not arrayed like one of these.

Wherefore, if God so clothes the grass of the field, which today is, and tomorrow is cast into the oven, shall he not much more clothe you, O ye of little faith? Therefore, take no thought in saying, what shall we eat? Or, what shall we drink? Or, Wherewithal shall we be clothed? (For after all these things do the Gentiles seek:) for your heavenly father knoweth that ye have need of all these things." Matthew 6:25-33

In other words, we must be assured that despite our needs, God has already made provision for them. In the 23rd Psalm, David affirmed that God is our provider. Because God is our shepherd, we will not want. In other words, all his needs are guaranteed to be met.

GOD IS THE PROTECTOR AND INSTRUCTOR

A father protects his children from harm. Scripture says that God guards and protects His children under the shadow of His wings (Psalm 91:1-4). Like a mother bird shelters her young ones, God is committed to providing shelter and covering for His children. The Bible says that God never slumbers nor sleeps in watching over us.

God is also our instructor. As an instructor, he shows us the way we ought to go and disciplines us to stay the course. He is the one who disciplines us to ensure we remain with His instruction. That is why we must understand that disciplining a child demonstrates love. Discipline introduces a child to a form of pain. But when you don't discipline a child, you expose him to greater pain. Pain is a sign that something is wrong or that a principle has been violated. Pain reminds us to adhere to instructions. Discipline, like the pains of life, teaches us that every time you break a principle, you face the consequences. God disciplines only those whom He loves. That enables you and I to share in His holiness (Proverbs 1:8, Hebrews 12:5-11).

In all these ways, God relates to believers as the ideal Heavenly Father described in scripture, who is always there to love, provide, protect, and guide His children. And that mirrors to us what a true earthly father should be. And that underscores the significant roles of fathers in the life of children.

1. A child's development

Fathers play critical roles in the healthy development of children. Children yearn for paternal love, support, nurturing, and guidance from infancy through adolescence and adulthood. Fathers who are positively involved in their children's lives have a profound, positive impact on their social, emotional, physical, and growth and general well-being. Many people have observed that children with engaged fathers display fewer behavioral problems, achieve higher academic success, and exhibit healthier self-esteem and confidence. Children whose fathers are available and play their fatherly roles effectively have more capacity to adapt in life.

You can predict a child's cognitive skills based on whether or not his father is available. Even toddlers whose fathers are better engaged with them show better intellectual development and attitude toward life. As for teenagers, when their fathers are involved in their lives, they show more confidence to learn and develop the personal skills required for life.

A father's presence and love are vital tools for shaping a child's mental and emotional wellbeing. Both boys and girls learn how to process their own emotions, how their father responds to situations, and how they express their emotions through different situations. Great fathers model critical lessons about managing anger, showing affection openly, working through sadness, and communicating inner emotional experiences. An available father can provide emotional support by attending his children's events and being present to cheer them up in times of accomplishment and console them for any area of failure or disappointment.

2. A father protects

Like our Heavenly Father, fathers protect their children. One of the most significant things a father's presence does is to ensure children feel safe and secure. A father's presence and involvement shield children from undue physical and emotional harm. Aside from emotional and psychological protection, fathers also provide physical protection, which assures children of safety despite anything that may be going on in their environment. But without this pretension made possible by a father's presence, children feel unsafe, anxious, and vulnerable. And for some others, they become open and the object of the assaults and attacks of evil people in the neighborhood.

3. A father is a teacher

A loving father is a skillful teacher of his children. A father must find a way to impart knowledge and wisdom to his children. Having gathered a wealth of experience from life, many truck and errors, he labors to transfer some of those life lessons to his children, to position them for advantage in the real world. And when they encounter challenges, he is always there to help them navigate their way. They gain the inspiration and confidence from him to confront and overcome some of life's darkest moments. His reassurance and encouragement allow them to stand tall as they navigate the dark maze of adult life. A father helps teach and nurture children to develop healthy social relationships. From parents, children learn how to interact with their peers and handle conflicts.

4. The provider

A father, like God, readily provides for his family. He is ready to go beyond the call of duty to meet the needs of his children and wife. Providing for the needs of the home is one of the most significant responsibilities of a father. As providers, fathers must work hard to meet their children's physical, financial, and material needs. By doing so, a father makes life comfortable for his wife and children and models the right attitude to life. He models the attitude of hard work, responsibility, and industry to his children, positioning them for a better future. Many fathers recognize that their children watch them closely and learn from their actions. Observation is one of the most powerful ways people learn.

5. The authority figure

The father is the authority figure in the home. That is probably the most important role of a father in the lives of the children, aside from providing for their materials and physical needs. If you study the divine order as revealed in the book of Ephesians, you will see the flow of authority from God himself down to the children. It starts with God, then Christ, the man, his wife, and finally his children. When this order is maintained, everything goes well. However, if this divinely established order is violated, everything begins to go haywire. According to the order, the children must submit to their mother as she submits to the father. But sometimes, when the father is absent, it becomes very challenging for the children to submit to a tighter mother. Of course, there are exceptions to the rule. However, more generally, the children, especially the sons, find it hard to submit to their mother without a father. This order of authority is why children are more likely to respond to their father's discipline than their mother's.

FATHERHOOD IS RESPONSIBILITY

Fatherhood did not originate from our culture, nor is it a biological accident; instead, it originated with God.

Fatherhood is a solemn calling bestowed on man by God. The amazing thing about this calling is that it carries a huge responsibility to the children, mothers, and society.

Children are a precious heritage that God entrusts into the care of fathers. In other words, God requires accountability from fathers on how they raise their children. Fathers are charged with the responsibility to nurture their children to greatness.

Visionary fathers view their children through a lens of possibility, seeking to inspire, teach, and prepare them for their glorious destinies. This is the main reason absentee fatherhood is very dangerous. When fathers are absent, uninvolved, or fail to play their role in the lives of the children, everything falls through for the children, mothers, and the entire society. Having a father who is not only present but actively and adequately involved in the life of the children from birth and through their adult life has negative ramifications on the wellbeing of the children.

We have considered some of the most significant roles of fathers to the children. But if you are still wondering whether fathers genuinely matter in the lives of children, look again. I want you to understand that a father's presence provides the shield that protects the children's future from the pitfalls that usually befall children without actively involved fathers. Fathers must, therefore, understand the significance of this and intentionally commit to showing up daily in their children's lives. And that is what true fatherhood is all about.

FATHERS TRULY MATTERS

Fathers are foundations. Without fathers, children will have no ground to build on and no firm footing to withstand the storms of life. What will you do without fathers? Fathers set the pace for what their children would eventually become. A father who is available and involved with his children becomes their pillar of strength. By being available, he can provide them with emotional support and the need to live and lead healthy adult lives. Without fathers, everything will go wrong, not just in the lives of the children but also with the mothers, the home, and society. The family is a miniature society. The state of society is a reflection of the state of the family. If the family is dysfunctional, society will be dysfunctional. The lack of actively involved fathers is one of the significant explanations for the many vices we have in society today. Most social vices we see today are perpetrated by people raised from dysfunctional homes. And I dare say that absentee fatherhood plays a major role in creating dysfunctional homes.

An engaged father provides robust support and a platform for a child's development. The steady presence of a father offers a safe harbor from which to explore dreams and weather storms that come along the way. A father's greatest gift is not necessarily meeting physical or material needs;

it is his companionship through life's joy and sorrow, guidance borne of experience, and the safety net of his unending devotion. When this is in place, a child's future is secured. Otherwise, that child is guaranteed a future full of despair, rejection, failure, and insecurity. Of course, no man can claim to meet all these needs perfectly, but a father's presence makes a lot of difference in the lives of the children.

True fatherhood is a fantastic opportunity to engage actively in a child's daily life and development. True fatherhood is everything. A father must, therefore, pay the price required to nurture their children; he must labor to become all he is meant to be for the betterment of the children, his wife, and the community. It's time to get to work!

Chapter Two
THE TRAUMA OF AN ABSENT FATHER

The absence of a father in a child's life can have profound and lasting consequences. Statistics show that children who grow up without an actively engaged father are more likely to experience a range of cognitive, emotional, and social problems that can lead to lifelong struggles. In the first chapter, we looked at some of the vital roles of fathers in positive child development and their impact on the child, wife, and society. In this chapter, we will focus on defining an absent father and the traumas that living without a father poses on a child's upbringing and progress in life.

An absentee father is a father who is not present in a child's life regularly and consistently. An absentee father is not present or involved with his child physically, emotionally, and otherwise. He does not spend substantial time with his children. And sometimes, even when physically present, he is detached, unavailable, and rarely interacts with his children meaningfully. An absentee father is a father who does not care about nor get involved with events, activities, and appointments related to his children. On the other hand, he does not provide regular, consistent financial support to help meet his children's basic needs. In essence, he is either absent or uninvolved in the lives of his children.

An insightful study has revealed that children living without their biological fathers were, on average, at least two to three times more likely to experience educational, health, emotional, and behavioral problems compared to children living with their biological parents (McLanahan, Tach & Schneider, 2013). According to the National Fatherhood Initiative (2022), children with absent fathers are more likely to become teenage parents or suffer from obesity, depression, and other emotional problems. That is disheartening!

TRAUMAS OF CHILDREN LIVING WITHOUT A FATHER

Children who grow up without actively involved fathers face significant emotional traumas and challenges. These traumas can profoundly impact a child's development and ability to form healthy relationships. Here are a few examples of traumas fatherless children are likely to experience:

1. **Low self-esteem issues**

Most children who have no present biological father often grow up thinking they are to blame for their father's absence. They seem to believe that it has something to do with them. As a result, this causes them to internalize negative messages about their self-worth. That is especially so during their adolescence stage of development. Having a father is crucial to maintaining healthy self-confidence. Without this, such children are bound to struggle with chronic low self-esteem. On the other hand, children with involved, loving fathers are significantly less likely to experience low self-esteem, identity crisis, poverty, or engage in criminal behaviors than those whose fathers were not present or involved in their lives.

2. **Trust and abandonment issues**

The trauma of losing a father or having an inconsistent father figure shatters a child's sense of security, making it extremely difficult for such children to have faith in others, including future partners. They usually think that intimate partners may leave them. Children of absent fathers often suffer from serious concerns about being abandoned or betrayed. That undermines future relationships.

3. **Cognitive disorder**

A father's absence significantly impacts a child's cognitive development and ability. In other words, it negatively affects a child's academic performance. This usually results from the lack of conversation and encouragement that only comes from a father. By the age of three (3), most children of absent fathers are probably already starting to show signs of dis-functionality, such as a lower intellectual ability, identity crisis, impulsivity, aggression, depression, anxiety, attachment disorders, and general destructive behaviors. Generally, children who grow up in father-absent homes are less able to complete their educational pursuits than those who grew up with their fathers. Sometimes, when you see a child struggling academically, don't be in a hurry to judge or say negative things about them because it may not be their fault anyway. Absentee fatherhood trauma may just be revealing itself.

4. Difficulty expressing emotions

Children need parental engagement to learn how to process complex emotions properly. Without involved fathers, children tend to repress their feelings, resulting in losing touch with their emotions and difficulty communicating needs. A father's absence denies children vital nurturing for healthy emotional development. This kind of trauma creates lasting mental health issues. As a result of this trauma, children find it challenging to form and maintain healthy and robust relationships with others.

5. High-risk behaviors.

The absence of a father is one of the strongest predictors that children will engage in high-risk activities such as drug and alcohol abuse, truancy, and criminal activities. When you see kids frequently acting out, it usually stems from unprocessed anger towards the missing father. Children also act out to get attention or gain acceptance from peer groups.

Children whose biological fathers are absent pose a very high risk of emotional and social challenges. I know this may sound scary, but boys raised without fathers are twice as likely to go to jail than those raised with present and involved fathers. For the girls with absent fathers, the story seems even more challenging, considering that they are three times more likely to get pregnant as teenagers (McLanahan, Tach & Schneider, 2013). That perpetuates the negative and disturbing cycle of fatherlessness from generation to generation.

Children who grow up without positively engaged fathers often struggle to form healthy relationships with peers while lots of others constantly grapple with low self-esteem issues, lacking the confidence to fully engage in life, embrace challenges, and emerge triumphant. That is disturbing, considering that these experiences and the conditions that go with them are not personal but eventually affect everyone around them, generations to come, and, by extension, the entire society.

MY JOURNEY

The trauma of absentee fatherhood can be outrightly overwhelming. Although the general statistics graphically paint a very gloomy portrait of the absent father, the personal impact of an absent father may only be fully appreciated by exploring the personal story of someone who has been through it. It can best be understood through a unique life experience like mine.

As I share my journey of absent fatherhood with you, I do hope that you not only see the trauma I had to go through growing up without my father, but you will also see the resilience that it takes to survive and thrive in spite of it.

Born in 1962 in a small town in Jamaica, I entered the world without a father. That is not to say that I fell from heaven (far from it). But what I am saying is that my father was absent. He had been absent long before the day of my birth. The circumstances surrounding my birth seemed somewhat "mysterious." And since no one would dare talk about the elephant in the room, it simply left me wondering about my father's whereabouts. And the result was that I became bitter and ungrateful.

Although my mother demonstrated love and care and provided for my needs as much as she could, the pressure and vulnerability that went along with growing up without a father did not let me appreciate all she did to make life as comfortable as it was. At least we were not homeless or begging for alms on the streets. Of course, things were not nearly as great as they were supposed to be, but I can confidently say that my mother did her very best to take care of me. At least, she did more than the average single mum, considering all the pressure and demands of such a status.

In all, it was not just my father's absence that troubled me the most, but the very fact that I could not seem to wrap my mind around any information about him or his reason for leaving my mother and me behind. The very thought of that was outrightly traumatizing.

Growing up, I always had this pressing question as to the whereabouts of my father. But since the answer wasn't immediately forthcoming, I decided to take it out on my mother despite all she did to take care of me. Rather than wait for the truth to come out eventually, I began to act out.

I became a rebellious child, deliberately refusing to follow my mother's instructions. And because there was no father figure in my life, no voice was strong enough to correct and keep me from going astray.

WHO HURTS THE MOST?

When fathers are gone, who gets hurt the most? The kids, of course! After that comes the mother. The mother has to care for the children as soon as the father is gone. She begins to work hard, doing multiple jobs to make ends meet. As a result, she may leave the home without any covering or protection.

The home becomes weak and divided when there is a lack of fatherhood. The enemy enters the home and destroys the mindset of the children, interfering with the divine order in the home. The children become rebellious to their mothers and, therefore, wayward. That is why many children have turned away from their homes and gone into the streets. And because nobody was there to guide them, they became prey to some evil father figures in the streets, who take them and counsel them to do the wrong things. That is how many children fall for the trap of the enemy and get derailed from their God-ordained destinies.

BACK TO MY STORY

The constant emptiness that I felt within drew me away from home and from a loving mother into the hands of dangerous street people whom I got involved with. Soon enough, the street became my lifestyle.

I was entirely on the street, drinking and smoking away my sanity. I was only 13 years old at that time. Later on, I ended up on drugs (marijuana, to be precise).

By the age of 15, going to 16, I was a full-blown gang member in the streets of Jamaica. That was the worst experience of my life. It was as though my entire life was captured and imprisoned in a dark tunnel. It affected me emotionally, physically, and mentally in no small way. I was almost losing my mind. My life would have been completely wasted if not for God's intervention. Thank God I found Jesus. Once I did, everything took a completely new turn.

Eventually, a pastor reached out to me, and that connection would later provide me with mentorship, support, and patient love. Through such a father figure, I developed a stronger relationship with God. And by God's enablement, I surrendered many destructive habits and began to heal from deep emotional wounds. My spiritual growth and walk with God culminated in my founding a church where lives are constantly transformed.

Later on, I found love and married the mother of my kids. And together, we love God and do his will for our lives. A once-lost son had found purpose and stability and has now become a source of inspiration to many other young kids. Today, I lead a rapidly growing congregation of young adult families brimming with hope. So, aside from raising a loving family of my own and pastoring the congregation God had committed into my care, I can also raise other kids with absent fathers with the hope of creating a better future for all of them. That responsibility is as exciting as it is demanding. But here is the beautiful part: The son of an absent father now raises other children who will carry forth a legacy with the potential to reshape lives for future generations. That is amazing!

MY MOTHER

I was later reconciled with my mother and lived with her until the day of her passing. But before her passing, she shared her own experience with my father and why she carefully kept it as a family secret. Of course, she opened up about that experience much later. She told me nothing about it (no matter how much I tried). I only found out about it when I was old. That was because when I got much older, got involved in church ministry, and started conducting deliverance services in the church, the deliverance message got at my mother one day, and she finally opened up and told me what had transpired between her and my father.

All along, I did not know that the experience that led to my conception was a one-night stand with a man she had known at the time. My mother was raped. This gruesome incident took place on a sad night sometime in the year 1962 when my mother was only 16 years old. Days, weeks, and months went by, and soon, she began to notice some strange bodily signs that pointed to pregnancy. She sincerely hoped her worst suspicion would turn out false, but when she eventually went to verify with a doctor, it turned out she was pregnant. Her worst suspicion had become her reality. It was the biggest shock of her life. And that would forever utter the trajectory of her life. Of course, she thought long and hard about exterminating the baby, but after much consideration, she decided to keep the pregnancy until she delivered. How a 16-year-old like she managed to survive that season of her life is something to think about. According to her, that was the worst season of her life.

My mother was a college student and was very proud, too. So she didn't want to talk about it. And because of what had happened to her, she became angry and bitter. She would have nothing to do with that man who raped her. She didn't want to mention his name at all. I guess she wasn't ready to risk the embarrassment that goes along with people knowing you had such a traumatic experience. She explained that from that night she was raped, she never saw that man again and did not know where he was to date.

Looking back, I could only imagine the level of pain she must have been through all those years when I would constantly bombard her with questions about my father's whereabouts. How could I have possibly put my mother through such emotional torture? "Oh my God!" I feel so sorry for all I had put her through.

IN SEARCH OF MY FATHER

Based on this newfound information, my daughter recently searched for further clues about locating my father. In the process, she had to run a DNA history test, which revealed a couple of things about my paternity and history. Firstly, the DNA history related to some people who are connected to my father. Some of them are presently living in New Jersey (USA).

When she made contact with them, one of my father's brothers confirmed that their brother was indeed living in the same area where my mother was at the time of the rape incident. So, it turned out that my father had died at over 100 years of age, long before my mother's demise. That simply implies that my father was way older than my mother.

Secondly, the DNA test revealed that my brothers and sisters live in Jamaica. Although my father is late, all his brothers and sisters are still alive. As a result of these recent findings, they want me to meet them so we can sit down and talk. They showed me his picture and said a lot about him.

Considering the circumstances that surrounded my birth, coupled with its traumatic impact on my mother and my upbringing, it is possible to continue to hurt and resent my father. However, he is already dead, yet because of the love of God in my heart, I was able not only to overcome the trauma but also to learn to embrace my (late) fathers. I felt relieved when I finally found out about my father and what had transpired between him and my mother.

And this is because, as a child of God, the Spirit of God has taken over my heart. I am open to anything. Of course, I'm unsurprised because I'm wrapped up in the Spirit of God. That is the reason I have no anger, no bitterness, or resentment towards my late father. The Spirit of God has shed His love abroad in my heart and has enabled me to keep my flesh under subjection. But in all, I am excited to finally know who my biological father was and what had transpired at my birth.

God has helped me to overcome every negative pain that could have resulted from such a traumatic experience. Today, I can use my knowledge and expertise to help not just kids but also fathers and mothers who could have been victims of similar situations. Although I have come to be free from the negative impact of absent fatherhood, it is critically important to understand how this experience can hurt and traumatize those who may share such an experience as mine.

The trauma of an absent father can be genuinely overwhelming not just for the children but for the woman left at home. I have shared my story to show you how traumatizing it can be to have to grow into adulthood without the loving arm, presence, and involvement of your father. So, whether you have had a similar experience or know someone who has had such a traumatic experience or not, we all have to appreciate the fact that it's not a good place to be. And whether you agree or not, the trauma that such people go through has a direct or indirect impact on all of us. The worst effect of these traumas is in their tragic capacity to perpetuate a cycle of paternal abandonment beyond the present generation.

Has your father abandoned you? Are you presently going through the trauma of an absent father? I want you to know that no matter the trauma you are facing as a result of an absent or uninvolved father, there is a way out for you in God. If you open your heart to God, you will not only be healed and delivered from the trauma but also be supernaturally empowered to lift others. Do not lose heart; do not give up, for light is at the end of the tunnel.

Chapter Three
WHY FATHERS LEAVE

When fathers leave home, they abandon their responsibility to their children, wives, and community. It is terrible for a father to abandon his family and head in another direction. The father's leaving home spells disaster for the whole family. Leaving your wife and children is against God's plan for marriage and family. The phenomenon of absentee fatherhood is a total departure from the norm; it is a departure from the scripturally ordained structure of the home.

Several Bible passages speak of the importance of a husband cleaving to his wife and not separating from her. The first and most crucial example is found in the second chapter of Genesis:

"Therefore shall a man leave his father and his mother, and shall cleave unto his wife: and they shall be one flesh." Genesis 2:24

The same scripture is quoted by Jesus in Matthew's gospel (Matthew 19:5), alluding to a scriptural principle of leaving and cleaving. As a man and husband, you must understand that you don't marry to leave; you marry to cleave. When you take a woman to the altar of marriage, you are committing to stick with her for the rest of your life. Therefore, when a father leaves, he violates his commitment to his wife and the children. Abandoning your family violates your sacred vows and duties, alters the dynamics of the home, harms the family, and goes against God's commands for marriage and caring for one's family.

God not only commands that a husband cleaves to his wife and, by extension, his children, but He commands husbands to love their wives as Christ loved the church. The Bible calls fathers to faithfulness and provision, not abandonment. Fathers must provide for and take care of their families. Walking out on them, therefore, goes against these responsibilities (1 Timothy 5:8). Abandoning your home for other options signifies breaking faith with the wife of your vow. When a husband breaks faith with his wife, leaving his children, he immediately paves the way for the total wreckage of the family, beginning with the children and then the wife.

By all standards, it is terrible to abandon our home. The Bible speaks very negatively about men and fathers forsaking their wives and children. It clearly describes the action of a husband who breaks faith with his wife as one covering his garment with violence.

"Malachi 2:16 For the LORD, the God of Israel, saith that he hateth putting away: for one covereth violence with his garment, saith the LORD of hosts: therefore take heed to your spirit, that ye deal not treacherously." Malachi 2:16

In other words, there is violence and harm that comes with abandoning one's family duties. In ancient biblical cultures, a man leaving his wife places her and her children in highly vulnerable situations since women lacked certain legal and economic protections at that time. It was an act that could bring oppression, injustice, and hardship.

However, it hits differently today, with a justice system prioritizing women and their children. The system of child support and all that goes with it sometimes puts women in a better position when fathers choose to leave. Unfortunately, all the systems put in place by the government to protect women and children will never be sufficient to cater to the deficiency and vulnerability that is usually created by the absence of a father. When fathers are absent, everything goes wrong, putting everyone involved in a negative situation.

Why would any reasonable father want to abandon his wife and children just like that? Why would you want to make your family go through such a traumatic experience? Why do many fathers leave their families and disappear into thin air? There are several reasons fathers leave home, abandon their families, and move on to other women or remain single. As we examine the example below, you will see some of the reasons fathers leave home, abandoning their wives and children:

FROM WEDDING BLISS TO TOTAL SEPARATION

Jenny and Mark met on a blind date set up by mutual friends. They hit it off right away, bonding over their love of Italian food, classic films, and a desire for a good life. After a beautiful courtship filled with romantic picnics in the park and cozy nights cooking dinner together, Mark proposed on a trip to Atlanta, and Jenny joyfully accepted.

On a sunny June day, surrounded by their closest family and friends, Jenny and Mark exchanged heartfelt vows under a floral archway, promising to love each other in sickness and health, for richer or poorer. The reception was filled with laughter, joyful dancing, and celebration of their new life together as husband and wife.

After Five blissful years together in a happy blur, Jenny and Mark welcomed a son and then a daughter and their family felt complete. Mark was thriving in his career in telecommunications, providing a comfortable life for his growing family. Little did he realize how short-lived his excitement would be.

When the tech bubble burst, Mark suddenly lost his lucrative management job. Jenny had left her teaching career years earlier to focus on raising the kids. After months of Mark struggling to find work, their financial situation became dire.

It was then that the loving wife he married seemed to transform before his eyes. Gone was the gracious, kind-hearted woman he fell in love with, replaced with someone stressed, short-tempered, and demanding. Of course, he picked up odd jobs doing yard work and waiting tables to provide for his family, but every effort he made did not impress his wife, who treated him with disdain.

Aside from ignoring his efforts, she constantly nagged at him. Her hurtful words toward Mark were far worse than dealing with their difficult financial situation. Over time, he became deeply depressed and felt completely trapped. Despite his religious faith urging him to keep his marital vows, Mark finally moved out, needing temporary relief. He didn't want to leave his children, but He had to find his footing somehow.

Leaving was a welcome idea for Mark, but soon, he would get involved with another woman and many other women. Meanwhile, the chances of ever reconciling with his wife dwindled and eventually were lost completely. What had started as a sweet dating story and wonderful wedding experience ended in a painful dissolution of everything they had built together.

Mark moved into a tiny apartment across town, taking odd jobs to afford the cheap rent. He started dating a woman named Tina, who worked at a nearby diner. She was newly divorced and had an outgoing, carefree attitude that Mark found refreshing after years of living in his marriage's tense, gloomy atmosphere.

For a while, Mark was happy—going out to eat, to movies and concerts afforded by his childless lifestyle, and Tina's company. But gradually, her youthful impulsivity began to take a toll on him. She would throw fits over small things and demand expensive gifts Mark couldn't afford. After catching Tina flirting one too many times, Mark broke it off.

Mark now found himself alone yet again. He tried finding solace in other fleeting relationships, but he only felt emptier and unfulfilled after each one inevitably crashed and burned. He couldn't help but think of his wife Jenny and the kids back home he missed seeing every day. The legal separation dragged on for over a year before Jenny reluctantly agreed to file for divorce.

On the day the divorce papers were finalized, Mark only felt sadness—not the relief he had hoped for. Jenny got the house and primary custody of the kids in the settlement. Pictures surfaced on social media showing Jenny's new boyfriend, Jim, moving into their old home. Jim seemed like a stable, upstanding guy, providing the father figure role Mark wished he could have maintained for his children.

Alone in his underfurnished apartment with takeout containers and unpaid bills, Mark pondered how he had found himself in this mess. If only he had been more supportive of Jenny's stress during their financial crisis instead of seeking escape. If only he had fought harder for their marriage before both said and did things, crossing lines that could never be uncrossed. But the past couldn't be undone. All Mark could do now was try to rebuild some sense of normalcy and pray he hadn't forever lost connection with the people he loved most.

The divorce was finalized, and Mark felt he had hit rock bottom. His tiny apartment could barely contain his grief, regret, and longing for his old life. On weekends with his kids, full of strained small talk, he put on a brave face while dying inside at the sadness in their eyes. His son acting out, his daughter withdrawn - and the news that Jenny was engaged to Jim just one year after the divorce.

Mark coped in unhealthy ways - drinking too much and pushing away well-meaning friends and until late one night, pulling into his parking spot at the apartment, narrowly missing hitting a woman taking out her trash in the adjacent alley. Her shouting shook him to the realization he had to make a change.

Later, Mark started going to counseling, dealing with years of repressed emotions. He opened up to his counselor, Anne, about the pain he felt over destroying his family and marriage. Anne helped him see that by taking responsibility and getting help, he was taking the first steps, despite starting late, toward becoming the man he wanted his children to know ultimately. Soon after, he started special meetings, getting sober and regaining clarity. As a result, he secured more steady work in tech support and lived a better quality of life. Unfortunately, he did life alone, without the presence of those he loved the most—his wife and children.

Although the Mark and Jenny story is a work of fiction, their experience shows why fathers leave home, abandoning their wives and children for options that might even hurt in the coming days and years.

Now, for Mark and Jenny, the constant nagging occasioned by the financial difficulty they both faced made him leave. For many other fathers, it could result from something else altogether. Here are a few reasons fathers leave home:

1. Financial Stress

Money issues occupy a critical role in causing conflicts in marriages. Some people have many reasons to believe that the top cause of crisis in marriages is finances or finances-related issues. If you find a couple in a conflict, chances are such a crisis has a financial undertone. The costs of raising children and maintaining the home can increase financial pressures in the home. Suppose the principal breadwinning father experiences a job loss, like, in the case of Mark and Jenny, or reduced income resulting from Company policies or a general downturn in the economy. In that case, a father may consider abandoning the family an appealing option. Now, while there is no legitimate reason for a father to leave his wife and children, we must acknowledge the financial presumption that goes along with raising a healthy family. Of course, some men even take on a second job to make ends meet, sometimes leaving them absent from family life. However, when the pressure goes beyond them, like in the case of Mark and Jenny, the father may leave for literal or emotional reasons. That is why a couple should be financially educated and have financial goals, strategic plans, and a clear budget to make things work. Couples must learn to upgrade their skills regularly to increase their income. Also, couples should consider creating reasonable time to engage in robust conversations regarding their finances.

2. Feeling Trapped or Suffocated

One of the most frequently cited reasons men give for leaving their families is a sense of losing their freedom. Depending on how they have patterned their life before getting married, coupled with a lack of adequate preparation for the many responsibilities of marriage, men may suddenly feel constrained by their newfound duties and responsibilities to their family life. As a result, they begin to desire to regain their independence.

The truth is, the responsibilities of a husband and father can be outrightly overwhelming sometimes. For some men, it is having to check in with a spouse, seeking her consent on some vital decisions you want to make, and getting them off. For others, it is coping with domestic activities like assisting the wife with the kids' activities and the other demands of being a husband. Sooner or later, the man feels like losing precious time to the family's several activities.

Sincerely, this can make some men feel trapped. That is especially so for men who probably had children at a young age before fully establishing their careers and interests.

Men who have already established their career path before marriage know what to expect from their spouse and the different marriage demands. Therefore, as the market comes along, they can adjust. However, men who have only recently discovered their career paths sometimes find it difficult to cope with the new demands of family life.

On the other hand, many young couples fail to define their union expectations properly. As a result, when marriage demands begin, they don't know how to manage it to prevent a major crisis.

As a result, couples need to consider building robust communication with each other, redefining their expectations, and making a solid commitment to make the sacrifices required to build their marriage. Another vital step couples can take is to make time apart where each person is engaged with their hobbies. That will allow both couples to take a break from their usual parental duties. On the other hand, a man can quickly identify what aspects of his marriage and home make him feel confined and find creative ways to express himself outside the home. That is equally true for the woman. A woman should have her private time sometimes to refresh herself and take a quick break from the demands of her home.

3. Lack of marital commitment and intimacy

Many relationships and marriages start all fired up, bustling with life. However, something seems to go wrong sooner or later, and the initial love and affection that brought the two invidious together wholly disappears. Often, people fail to realize that the feeling of affection, as powerful as it may be, is not sufficient to sustain a marital relationship, especially during trying times. Couples who intend to stick together over the long haul must go beyond the usual feeling of love to the commitment of love.

Aside from the commitment from a deep-seated understanding of the marriage covenant, couples must consciously labor to build intimacy and friendship with each other long before children begin to come. Otherwise, once children show up, they are bound to change the dynamics of the marriage.

Suppose you fail to develop intimacy with your spouse before the demands of careers, parenting, and daily life begin to get in the way. In that case, you are putting your marriage at risk of possible separation. In such times, most fathers consider leaving home as a way to escape the overwhelming pressure facing them.

However, where intimacy and commitment already exist, couples find common ground to realign themselves, thereby saving their marriage. On the other hand, the lack of intimacy can force some fathers to seek intimacy someplace else. That is so unfortunate. Improving intimacy requires carving out regular quality time together. A time devoid of every form of distraction. Partners should prioritize communication, empathy, trust, and affection, not just family responsibilities and logistics.

4. Infidelity

Another reason fathers seem to depart is infidelity. Cheating on your spouse is sure to break your marriage. Of course, some marriages survive it. Of course, many women are aware of the fact that their husbands are cheating on them, yet they stay on, trusting that they will eventually turn a new leaf. Of course, it often doesn't end up as they hoped. Now, as bad as it is for a man to be flirting around with a woman other than his wife, it is even worse to see a situation where the woman is the one flirting around with other men. That is such a sad experience for any man.

Usually, when extra-marital affairs come to light, betrayal and loss of trust frequently overturn the marriages, especially if the straying partner shows no remorse or a commuted effort to change for the better. For some people, rather than fix the mess they have created, unfaithful fathers often forge new lives and abandon their first family instead. That should never happen to any couple, especially if both profess faith in Jesus Christ. Your marriage bed should remain undefiled and reflect God's righteousness and integrity.

To prevent infidelity would require mutual nurturing of intimacy and communication in the marriage. However, both parties must establish relationship priorities and boundaries. Without well-defined boundaries, even the best of good intentions ends only as wishful thinking with many disappointments as the outcome. If, in any case, cheating does occur, both parties should engage a qualified and experienced counselor. Extensive counseling is meant to facilitate forgiveness between couples. Many counselors would strongly suggest you file for divorce should the continued affairs continue unabated. Even the Bible seems to leave room for the dissolution of such marriage ( ).

5. Starting a New Family

When God instituted marriage, His intention was for one man to stick to his wife until the event of death eventually separated them. A father, therefore, should pay the price to build his family. Unfortunately, some fathers leave existing children and spouses to begin families anew with different women. This ultimate abandonment results from other factors, as mentioned in this chapter. Some fathers often justify such a step to seek personal happiness. That is the reason maturity is significant in marriage. Maturity demands that you put your spouse and children above your interests. But because many people are immature, they tend to be selfish and seek their interests. And when a father gets involved with another woman, it automatically shifts focus and resources away from first kids and family. Couples must, therefore, labor to strengthen their family bond by maintaining openness in communication. However, if a new family is eventually allowed to fester, there is little hope of reconciling the first one without the dissolution of the new bonds. Even then, trust and emotions suffer permanent damage.

There are many more reasons why fathers may leave home reasons, such as substance abuse, mental health challenges, or other unforeseen circumstances. However, regardless of what may be or how appealing an option to leave, abandoning one's wife and children can scarcely be justifiable. Fathers must seek grounds for reconciliation and solutions, no matter how complicated the situation. Furthermore, every father must be strong enough to withstand the pressure from different negative life scenarios.

When this becomes the norm, every wife or child can rest, knowing that regardless of what happens along life's journey, their father will be right there for them.

In any case, both parties must invest effort in ensuring they stick together through the vicissitudes of life. And even when separation occurs temporarily, both parties must be willing to go the extra mile in coming back together, realizing the impact a total separation could have on their children. In doing so, couples protect themselves and their children and cover the coming generations.

Chapter Four
THE STRUGGLES OF SINGLE MOTHERS

When a marriage dissolves unexpectedly, a woman's life seems to fall apart like a pack of cards. A new world opened up for her, a world she had never imagined before that time, in which nothing would be the same again. That world is the world of single motherhood. She may have been to court, pressed charges, and even won the case. She may have gotten every resource turned over to her, yet her new status will forever haunt her like a lion running after its prey. In other words, regardless of how things play out, that woman will forever be thrown into the unfashionable world of single motherhood.

Many people get involved with marriage or business and need to consider what it would be like should unexpected things happen. Of course, we are faith people, and it just doesn't cross our minds that negative situations could arise,

especially when nothing of that sought seems to be anywhere close to happening. And make no mistakes: if you continue to imagine negative things, you will eventually attract them into your life. The Bible makes us understand that our lives usually go in the direction of our thoughts (Hebrews 11:15).

But as much as we love to think that no negative thing can ever happen to us, it does make sense to be prepared for anything and everything that may arise because as long as you are alive, you will encounter challenges. The rule of thumb would be: Expect the best but prepare for the worst.

Of course, no one enters marriage expecting a sudden breakup, separation, or divorce. A woman does not wake up expecting her husband and the father of her lovely children to suddenly walk away from her and the children. And so, when such things happen, most people are not only shocked but also caught unprepared.

We all must understand that unexpected and unpleasant things sometimes happen in life. Think of those heart-breaking experiences that many couples face or that highly disappointing and tragic moment people meet, and you will understand what I am talking about. Now, whether it is with a father leaving home or scenarios like what my mother went through, the absence of a father leaves the woman in a very vulnerable state.

Sometimes, we find a woman who is only playing a supportive role to her husband, and all of a sudden, she becomes the sole breadwinner of the house. And when a mother assumes the role of a man and father, she is forced into untold struggles beyond her wildest imagination, since she was not originally designed or equipped to do so. And that is the travail of a single mother.

Researchers have established that single mothers face severe emotional, mental, economic, and social challenges—all of which my mother battled in the years following her rape, teenage pregnancy, and the loss of touch with my father. But before we get into that, let us pause to draw a portrait of a single mother.

PORTRAIT OF A SINGLE MOTHER

A single mother is a woman raising children independently without a spouse or partner. Single mothers may have become parents through different life circumstances - some may have chosen to adopt or undergo fertility treatments to have a child while being yet unmarried. Some may be widowed, and some may have gone through a divorce or separation. Regardless of how they became single mothers, these women take on the full responsibility and challenges of raising children independently.

Single mothers come from all walks of life and backgrounds. They can be any age, race, ethnicity, socioeconomic status, or education level. The one thing connecting all single mothers is that they are parenting without daily physical, emotional, and financial support of a spouse or partner. That often makes the responsibilities and stresses of parenting exponentially more demanding.

WHY WOMEN BECOME SINGLE MOTHERS

Here are a few key reasons women may become single mothers: The first is divorce. The divorce rates suggest around 40-50% of marriages in the U.S. end in divorce. After a divorce, mothers are often awarded physical and legal custody of children. Some single mothers are made as a result of not being legally married before having children. For instance, in America, About 40% of children are born to unwed mothers. Some women choose to have children independently, depending on when they can find a suitable partner. That is increasingly becoming common in certain Western cultures.

Others become single mothers when the father of their kids suddenly walks out on them on account of an unresolved disagreement, which ends in separation.

Some women will even go ahead to adopt other people's children and raise them as theirs. Many people may not want to go through the process and stress of having to get married, get pregnant, and painfully bear their children, so they opt for other, more accessible options like adoption. It is reported that 25% of adoptions in the U.S. are by single parents.

But regardless of the reason, single mothers often do not initially expect or plan to raise such children independently. But just like the saying goes, "necessity is the mother of inventions," and so through necessity and resiliency, these single mothers put their children first and try to make it work. However, that is often at a significant cost on their part.

Every single day in America, Europe, and around the world, a single mother gropes under the massive burden of having to cater for her family's needs alone. Apart from the financial, physical, and social impact it has on her, she has a substantial psychological baggage to carry around every day of her life. That is rather unfortunate!

1. **The Emotional and Mental Toll**

One of the most significant issues for women, generally, is emotional challenges. The original makeup of women predisposes them to emotional issues. It becomes even more critical when such emotional problems result from a bad relationship. When a relationship or marriage goes sour, the woman is the worst hit emotionally.

When a father abandons his union and children and leaves,

the woman is suddenly thrust into a parenting role meant for two. In other words, women begin to play the roles intended for both men and women.

Unfortunately, those roles can be overwhelming because she is trying to fill the shoes of both mother and father. As a result, he begins to grapple with an onslaught of powerful emotions such as - grief, anger, shock, fear, and, in many cases, guilt. That throws such a woman into perpetual worry and anxiety, especially about how she would provide for the kids. That is especially true when the woman has no tangible and dependable source of likelihood.

One of the reasons this can be very emotionally draining is the feeling that they can no longer devote as much time and energy to the children as they would like. Women in this condition can quickly get annoyed, impatient, and reactive with their kids due to being overburdened, leading to further emotional turmoil. Without the support of a spouse to share responsibilities or reassure them during difficult times, many single mothers internalize intense feelings of failure and self-doubt. As the burden increases, it becomes challenging for them to concentrate on their duties at work, leading to inadequate emotional response at the workplace. When this happens, such a person cannot perform at her maximum, leading to other challenges that would boomerang her emotions. They are broken inside, with their self-esteem badly beaten, leading to a loss of self-confidence, and in extreme cases, mental health challenges could even ensue.

2. Economic Hardship

Nothing can be more challenging for a single mother than the pressure of having to take up the financial responsibility of the home. Of course, the man is supposed to send support regularly in the case of a divorce. Still, it is always different from being available and having to bear the financial responsibilities of the father of the house. It is very challenging without a substantial income capable of catering to the family's basic needs.

As a loving mother, she takes responsibility for meeting the family's financial needs, but despite her best efforts to push forward, the stark reality of poverty soon hits. And because she earns less, it becomes nearly impossible to bear the burden. The truth is that constant financial distress endured while raising children as the sole provider frequently condemns single mothers to lifelong poverty.

The early loss of working years to cater for the young children, coupled with lower average wages for women, totally destabilizes a single mother, making it nearly impossible for her to accumulate any form of assets or even retirement savings. This seemingly systematic income insufficiency further limits her ability to pursue higher education or job training, which could increase her earnings potential later.

All efforts to stay financially afloat drive her further into debt and financial difficulty. For some older singles, this could end in total bankruptcy. And that means they would remain impoverished into their more senior years. That is the reason a lot of single mothers have had to be entirely dependent on family or government welfare to survive.

3. Changes to Social Status & Relationships

Social connections and relationships are significant assets not just in life but also in recovering from a crisis. A person with viable relationships is more likely to recover faster from a setback than someone lacking them. Relationships are generally that powerful. Unfortunately, that is one luxury that is not available to many single mothers.

On top of economic and emotional hurdles, single mothers must adapt to changes in their social status and relationships. As a single mother, not only are you left alone to bear your financial needs and those of your children, you are left with a substantial social burden. You are left to grapple with social isolation.

Single mothers usually do not have time for a personal life outside of work and their many parenting duties. Their seemingly extreme busyness causes friendships and general social life to disappear completely. A single mother finds engaging with friends, colleagues, and even her extended family is challenging. She hardly has any time to spare for dating or anything like that. The bigger problem is that often, this lack of positive social connections can lead single mothers to feel increasingly lonely, withdrawn, and disconnected from society. It may also limit the social development of the children since single mothers have fewer opportunities to facilitate their children's interaction with other adults and kids. The ultimate implication of this chain reaction is that social isolation prevents single mothers from getting the support and opportunities that could ease their load and, in turn, improve the quality of life for them and their children.

4. Psychological Trauma

The daily rigors of single parenthood can have a tremendous psychological impact on single mothers. Mothers raising children alone are constantly compelled to do many things simultaneously and with limited resources. They often have to combine their work life with their family time, school activities, and household maintenance. The tremendous mental strain that ensues from this can sometimes evolve into severe, chronic psychological trauma with lasting impacts on their mental health. The constant demands often serve as a source of toxic stress. As a result, they cannot find the time needed to cater for themselves adequately. Without much time for self-reflection or healing, this unresolved grief, anxiety, guilt, anger, and loneliness fester. That usually increases the risk for substance abuse and clinical mood disorders. It is a well-known fact that single mothers exhibit dramatically higher rates of prescription drug addiction, alcoholism, and personality disorders that remain ongoing issues even after their children grow up.

5. Damaged Relationships with Children

The overwhelming demands single mothers contend with frequently get in the way of forging deep emotional bonds with children. The vast demands single mothers face often obstruct the opportunity to form a deep bond with their children. Quality time and emotional availability become far-fetched because of all the challenges associated with single parenthood and the ongoing needs of a household without a partner. At this point, we have to prioritize stability over deep family bonds. The result is that the children suddenly become resentful of their mother. Children of single mothers often blame their mother for the father's absence or the burdens brought on them by his lack of involvement. With all these arguments about who is to blame, family members are further drawn apart, resulting in constant family feuds. Research shows these fractured relationships don't just end but continue into the next generations.

Children who felt abandoned by a single mom unable to attune to their needs often mature to similarly withdraw from their kids emotionally while criticizing their partners. Mothers must intentionally prioritize quality time with their children. They must decide to lend a listening ear to grieving children without judging them. Children must be allowed to express their feelings, without which these feelings may implode, causing more significant trouble shortly. On the other hand, the children must show empathy to their mother, considering what she must endure to care for everyone. Children must appreciate the sacrifice of their single mothers.

Mothers are a fantastic group of people. No matter how thinly stretched they get, they always made time to help their children with homework, clean them up when necessary, and soothe their other heartaches. Above all, their love for their children often gave them the strength and courage to keep fighting, even when they felt utterly spent.

RESILIENCE AND DETERMINATION

Being a single mother is very challenging, but as difficult as it may seem, a single mother must never allow herself to be disadvantaged by her new status or let it stop her from raising her children and nurturing their glorious destinies. As a single mother, the stress of being one should never stop you from discerning your children's future and paying the price to bring it to light.

A recent study carried out by Professor Alicia VanOrman of Brigham Young University in 2018 on single motherhood shows that single mothers endure more depression, stress, and psychological distress compared to mothers living with their partners. However, most single mothers demonstrate incredible resilience despite inadequate social support. Many single mothers have a story of resilience and courage despite substantial physical, financial, and psychological burdens.

Despite all the challenges and burdens of being a single mother, many single mothers have proven that you can raise healthy and highly successful kids.

Throughout history, single mothers have raised their children to greatness and influence. In almost every field, some of the world's greatest minds were raised by single mothers. From the former president of the USA, Barack Obama, to Oprah Winfrey, LeBron James, Justin Bieber, J.K. Rowling, and many others, single mothers raised all of them. Of course, if you meet them in person, they can tell you a bit about their resilience, tenacity, and determination journey. Their determination has proved to be their greatest weapon amid all the stress and challenges of being single mothers.

Faced with such severe trials, many women might have crumbled beneath the pressure. Yet amazingly, as the pressure consistently mounts, many single mothers gradually develop coping strategies that help them alleviate this intense stress and anxiety. Whether lighting candles, reminiscing their great past experiences, or getting partially involved with early morning running to prepare themselves mentally for each difficult day or whatever they chose, they found a way to remain afloat. For me, this is the spirit of single motherhood. And that is the attitude it takes to survive and thrive as a single mother.

Without strategic intervention, the destructive impacts of an absent father on single mothers could be far-reaching.

It could end up creating lifelong adversity. However, with dogged commitment, determination, and resilience, the possibility of ending the damaging cycle and creating a thriving future ahead arises. Single mothers must be rugged, challenging, and robust. They must choose forward-thinking instead of victim mentality, determination instead of apathy, and resilience instead of vulnerability. A single mother must never crumble under pressure because she might be the hope for the next generation of children. As challenging as it may seem, that is the only way forward.

Chapter Five

HEALING FROM ABSENT FATHER'S WOUND

Tim stared at the graphs and charts littered across his home office desk. As a data analyst, he often took solace in numbers and statistics, finding comfort in their predictability. This time, it was not about the graphs but the present marital unrest in his home.

His wife, Clara, had grown distant in recent months. Their once warm conversations had been strangely replaced by cold silence. Times of intimacy were even becoming rare. Not realizing what had changed, Tim started to blame himself. Perhaps he needed to be more attentive to Clara's needs or said "I love you" enough.

In his darker moments, Tim couldn't help but wonder if Clara regretted their marriage. And because they'd been together since college, he thought she may have grown bored and now questioned if they had married too young. Of course, he wondered what he could do to reignite the spark.

As he quietly agonized over the demise of his marriage, he couldn't help but think of his father. His dad had left when Tim was just five years old, exiting without any explanation. One moment, he could see and talk with his father; the next, he vanished from Tim's life altogether.

Tim always felt a gaping hole in his father's absence that no one else could fill. When he married Clara, he had hoped to find the stable family life that had eluded his childhood. And for many years, he did - until recently. Now, it felt like everything he had desperately tried to hold together was suddenly coming apart.

Tim worried that his flawed history with an absent father was catching up to him. Perhaps he was destined to mimic his dad - to abandon those he loved. Or even worse, he abandoned himself. "How could this be?" What was he going to do?" He mused.

The more Clara pulled away, the more Tim's insecurities and wounds festered. Often, he tried suppressing memories of his dad packing bags late at night, closing the door silently. That was what he saw as young. Although baffled then, he did not know what to do or say. But the more Clara retreated emotionally, the louder Tim's childhood wounds seemed to scream.

One evening, Clara gently suggested they seek counseling. But Tim didn't immediately oblige. His first instinct was to recoil, insisting that nothing was wrong. He worried that admitting troubles would mean he had failed Clara in providing the very stability his fractured childhood lacked. But Clara took his hand, looking into eyes that mirrored the hurt of his five-year-old self, still lamenting his father's exit. At that moment, Tim knew he had to stop the coverup and face the man in the mirror. He knew he had to stop running from his very own shadow.

Over the following months, a wise counselor helped Tim to say words to the wounds that had silenced him all these years. And now his marriage with Clara was at stake. He had to quickly admit that while he couldn't change his past, he could change how he allowed it to shape his behavior and future. He doesn't have to remain a prisoner to his old pain when he could simply choose to own up to it and allow himself time to heal.

With Clara by his side, Tim could unlock aspects of his childhood he had locked away for decades. Together, they embraced God's healing grace. And though Tim will never forget his dad's absence, he refuses to let such old wounds sabotage and define his present reality. He chose to continue to do life with Clara.

MANY ARE WOUNDED

As God's beloved children, we are designed for connection—to love and be loved within healthy family relationships. But what happens when a father's wound occurs? The parent-child bond is damaged, and the resulting pain runs deep, often shaping one's identity and ability to receive love. As we can see in the case of Tim and Clara, many men (both young and old) are just as wounded. Like Tim, they might not realize how deeply hurt they are by their absent father until later on in life. Unfortunately, many people have had to repeat the mistakes of their absent fathers simply because they were still carrying the wounds themselves. What could be more painful than for a child to grow up without the caring and nurturing arm of his father?

When a father leaves, the children are left grappling with several debilitating wounds, just like Tim. Although these wounds may appear invisible, they have huge spiritual, emotional, mental, and physical ramifications. When fathers leave, not only are the women hurt and broken, as we have seen in a previous chapter, but the children are often deeply wounded. An absentee father's wound usually manifests itself in several ways.

This chapter will explore the wounds associated with an absent father and how to find healing and wholeness in God the Father. Along the line, we will discover the transforming power of forgiveness and its impact on reconciling the hearts of fathers and their children. By applying the power of forgiveness and other principles revealed in this chapter, you can overcome every absentee father's wound you may be struggling with right now. Finding healing for emotional wounds is an internal work that requires courage, vulnerability, and rewiring of emotional patterns. But after all is said and done, a wounded soul will be transformed to live a more fulfilling life.

WOUNDED BY MY FATHER

Absentee fathers' wounds refer to the psychological, emotional, and behavioral injuries experienced by children who grow up with fathers who are physically or emotionally absent from their lives for significant periods. These psychological issues stop people from being their best, maximizing their potential, and living fulfilled lives. Children raised without their fathers often struggle with believing they are loved and accepted. And this can grossly sabotage true success later in life. That is why these issues need to be resolved in time. These wounds are simply the outer manifestations of an inner deficiency. Like physically ill people, wounded people are emotionally sick. Here are a few examples of an absentee father's wounds:

1. A deep Feeling of Abandonment

As children who are separated from their father begin to grow and become totally aware of their father's obvious absence, the first thing that happens is that they suddenly start to see themselves as being intentionally abandoned by their father. They begin to feel let down by the one person who is supposed to love them truly. As a result, this feeling of unworthiness establishes an early pattern for unstable, inconsistent relationships throughout life. Research shows that the lingering distress of abandonment by one's father often manifests later as separation anxiety, clinginess with partners, and profound grief when relationships end (Payne 2011). That is the reason why this wound cuts deep.

2. Difficulty in giving or receiving love

Men and women raised in homes without paternal emotional availability usually demonstrate greater lifelong struggle to establish stable romantic bonds. That is unfortunate because they discover they are incapable of love at a point where they should find love. In other words, they cannot give or receive love from others. They also find it challenging to communicate affection.

A wounded person is like a broken vessel; a fractured vessel cannot hold stuff or retain what is put into it. As soon as you pour in any liquid, it simply flows out. It's not that the container does not want to retain its content; it simply cannot. That is precisely the case with the children of an absentee father. What that does is that such people grow into full adulthood without any significant romantic relationship. And even when such relationships begin to fester, they tend to break it.

More so, emotional intimacy must have an internal template

to rest. This template is the outcome of a foundation laid through a healthy father-child relationship, which is only available to kids whose fathers are emotionally and physically present. If this is missing, you find adults always seeking validation from others.

That explains why many people are so needy and vulnerable in relationships. But the good news is that those deprived of such paternal support can be healed with focused and intentional efforts over time. They can become whole enough to cultivate deep, intimate relationships now and in the future. That is also why it is essential to identify these tendencies earlier in life so that proper care can be taken to solve them.

3. The feeling of rejection

Another very significant wound inflicted by absent fathers is the wound of rejection. Rejection seems to be one of the worst of all the wounds of an absentee father. Having been seemingly rejected and abandoned by someone duty-bound to love them, children grow up grappling with the feeling of rejection. The rejection they once received from their father's abandonment registers like a program in their subconscious, thereby controlling the way they feel about themselves in relation to others. Rejection is a sickness of the soul which manifests as different behavioral tendencies. The feeling of rejection usually snowballs into loneliness; loneliness becomes self-pity, self-pity becomes misery, misery becomes depression, and depression becomes despair and hopelessness, leading to suicide or death. That is why rejection is very terrible. If rejection is not identified early enough and handled appropriately, it can ruin any life.

4. Gender identity struggles

A general struggle or confusion with one's sex is a huge sign that someone is suffering from a deep wound resulting from the absence of a father. That is especially so for young boys. One of the vital things a father must do is to help a child identify who they are in terms of sex. That is done simply through modeling. However, if the father is absent, boys do not have a clear male role model to look at to help them understand who they are. And with the current global confusion about sexual orientation, it becomes even more challenging for all those with absent fathers. Of course, rare cases of strange feelings and orientations result from other factors. Still, most of these confusions stem from some form of emotional sickness that could have been avoided if fathers were available to model the correct identity. That must be done early enough before they are corrupted with the new and strange sexual orientations.

5. Lack of self-confidence

Another major wound that results from an absent father is the erosion of self-worth. Nothing can make a child feel unworthy as not having a loving father who is physically and emotionally present for him. It is nearly impossible to stand tall when the most important people in your life have treated you as worthless and unimportant to them. Growing up without the love, care, and protection that comes only from a father is a big deal when it comes to developing a healthy self-worth. When a father walks away or is technically absent for an extended period, that is usually the image it paints on the canvas of children's hearts. And when that is the case, children grow into adulthood with little or no self-worth.

6. General bad behavior

The absentee father's wound leads to general destructive behaviors. Studies show that children with absent fathers tend to have more disciplinary issues, aggression, hyperactivity, and delinquent behavior as they grow older. That may be related to unmet needs for a father's discipline and guidance. Usually, fathers are the ones who discipline their children. A lot of cultures no longer accept such disciplinary measures. And that explains the level of waywardness and lack of control we see in children born in many Western cultures today. Children want to be their parents. They don't want anyone to discipline or hold them accountable for their actions. When you closely consider some of the laws that have been put in place, you will see why it has become nearly impossible to discipline young kids.

Other kinds of wounds include high impulsiveness, substance abuse, anger and resentment, perfectionism, fear of trust, and depression/anxiety disorders. All these wounds can destroy a child's chances of living a successful life. Every day of our lives, we find people who, though gifted with rare gifts, yet are crippled inside, virtually unable to get themselves to take the steps that can bail them out, all because of some of these wounds. There are more emotional cripples than physical cripples sitting in wheelchairs all around the world.

There is healing for you.

But the good news is that healing is possible! All around us are people who look healthy and whole. Nothing seems to be physically wrong with them, but like the Bible woman of the issue of blood, they are constantly bleeding inside. I mean, deep within their soul. If you have been wounded emotionally as a result of your father's leaving you, and you are wondering if there is a way out, look no further because there is great hope for you.

God did not only promise to heal our physical bodies but also our hearts and emotions. In many places, the word of God alludes to this fact. When Jesus came out of the wilderness of temptation, having been supernaturally empowered by the Holy Spirit, He boldly declared that He had been anointed to heal the brokenhearted.

"And there was delivered unto him the book of the prophet Esaias. And when he had opened the book, he found the place where it was written; The Spirit of the Lord is upon me, because he hath anointed me to preach the gospel to the poor; he hath sent me to heal the

brokenhearted, to preach deliverance to the captives, and recovering of sight to the blind, to set at liberty them that are bruised." Luke 4:17-18

Another phrase the Bible uses for this condition is "a wounded spirit." (Proverbs 18:14). A wounded spirit is the same as a broken heart. The brokenhearted are simply those wounded inside. That tells us that many are bleeding heavily inside their soul, hoping for God's healing power.

On the other hand, we see all through the earthly ministry of Jesus that he not only healed people's bodies but also made them whole. The phrase being made whole is littered throughout the scripture. When people were healed, it meant that the spiritual undertone of their ailment was first dislodged, resulting in their physical healing. However, when people are made whole, it means that whatever was physically missing was either replaced or made complete, including being emotionally healed.

GO BEYOND THERAPY

The wounds of an absent father may require meaningful therapy and support to heal. Many people's first response to these wounds is therapy. Of course, therapy is an effective way to get through emotional and psychological wounds; however, some wounds are so deep that only God can heal them. God's word, energized by God's power, is the only instrument capable of traveling deeply into our human nature and constituents and correcting wrong things. The scripture tells us that God's word can cut through the diving asunder between our soul and spirit (Hebrew 4:12). Only words energized by the Holy Spirit can do that. The words of a therapist can only go so far. Many therapists are doing a great job, but we must learn to go beyond therapy to surrender our souls and spirit to the power of the Holy Spirit. That way, we can be supernaturally healed and made completely whole from the inside out.

DISCOVER OUR HEAVENLY FATHER'S LOVE

To experience inner healing, you must get to know the father's love. I am talking about the love of our Heavenly Father, which he demonstrated by giving up His son to die for our sins. You can't give or receive love until you experience the father's love. God is not just our creator; He is our father. In the book of Psalms, He is referred to as the father of the fatherless (Psalms 68:5)

The incredible thing is that our Heavenly Father offers us what an earthly father cannot offer. He provides a nurturing environment where the fatherless can embrace their identity as chosen sons and daughters. His spirit fills those who feel abandoned and rejected. In other words, God's reassuring love is always there for you regardless of what you may have been through. He is always there to heal the brokenhearted. All you need to do is to open up to His compelling love.

I realize that a fatherless child often unconsciously puts up walls when someone attempts to get close and show care or affection. The reason is because they don't want to be betrayed again. But as you fellowship with God through His word and spirit, these walls are gradually broken down, and you experience inner healing.

THE PLACE OF FORGIVENESS

Sometimes, all you need to do to experience healing is to forgive. You might feel hurt by your absent father. Of course, bitterness towards fathers is often felt to be justified. However, scripture reveals the negative impact of unforgiveness on our spiritual and physical health (Hebrews 12:15). You cannot afford unforgiveness. As we fully receive God's forgiveness towards us, it empowers us to forgive others, including our absent fathers. (Matthew 18:21-35). God cannot forgive you if you refuse to forgive others. Remember, as long as you are holding someone down, you are holding yourself. True forgiveness frees the offended while acknowledging wrongs committed. When we release another from judgment, we choose to extend the same grace God shows toward our sin (Colossians 3:13). Forgiveness is accessed through a relationship with God. As He reveals His unwavering love towards us despite our flaws, we become empowered to see others through the eyes of compassion.

EMBRACE RECONCILIATION

And when the opportunity presents itself, we must be ready for reconciliation. If a father decides to return, whether wholly or partially, you must be willing to embrace and reconcile with him. That is the manifestation of the spirit of Elijah, which is promised to be released in the last days. The prophetic promise in Malachi indicates that there will be a reconciliation of the hearts of fathers and children across generations:

"And he will turn the hearts of fathers to their children and hearts of children to their fathers..." Malachi 4:6

This same Spirit of Elijah was what restored the Israelite people in the past (Ezekiel 36:26-27). And if He did it before, He will do it again. And one of the ways God transmits the spirit of Elijah is through His ordained ministers. God still moves through faithful mentors and ministers to broker healing between generations within families. As fathers and children humble themselves through the reconciliation process, their hearts reopen toward one another, and healing takes place. Hallelujah!

The father's absence inflicts many wounds on both children and adults, causing them untold pain and frustration in life. But with the principles we have shared, healing can be obtained. A wounded soul is a sick soul, and until such a person is healed, they will not only not function well in life, but they will also keep hurting others. Hurting people hurt others. But as they embrace the love and grace of God, healing becomes inevitable. God's grace is always available to heal and deliver, not just those who are physically sick but also those grappling with emotional and psychological sicknesses. Let's go for it!

Chapter Six
BREAKING THE CURSE OF ABSENTEE FATHERS

The absence of fathers in families can have tremendous negative consequences that travel through generations. People who grow up without their father's presence tend to replicate their father's absentee behaviors. The Bible speaks extensively about the vital role of fathers and how they are called to actively love, lead, discipline, and spiritually nurture their children (Deuteronomy 6:4-9, Ephesians 6:4). When fathers are disconnected or absent, it creates a vacuum in the family and wounds the hearts of children. In the previous chapters, we looked at the different sounds that can arise from absentee fathers and how to find healing.

However, it is very crucial to note that as terrible as it is to experience the wounds from an absentee father, it is not nearly as awful as having to watch it perpetuated to the next generation. Unless intentional intervention interrupts this seemingly vicious cycle of absentee fatherhood, it will most likely be perpetuated to the next generation. The Bible makes us understand that the sins of the fathers eventually become the sins of the children, rippling further unto the third and fourth generations:

> *"Thou shalt not bow down thyself to them, nor serve them: for I the LORD thy God am a jealous God, visiting the iniquity of the fathers upon the children unto the third and fourth generation of them that hate me." Exodus 20:5*

According to some statistics, children of absent fathers are far more likely to become absent parents themselves than children who are raised by their fathers, thus perpetuating the same emotional distance, wounds, and dysfunctional behaviors from generation to generation. In other words, absentee fathers often beget absentee fathers in the next generation. The following statistics reveal the transgenerational nature of absentee fatherhood:

- American boys who grew up with absent dads are over twice as likely to become young, absentee fathers compared to boys raised by both parents.

- At least 20% of absentee fathers were themselves raised without a biological dad present.

- 70% of high school dropouts go on to become absentee dads. Missing school is itself 2.5 times more likely for fatherless boys.

- Sons of absentee fathers are three times more likely to be incarcerated, creating forced separation. Prior inmate status doubles the odds of abandoning kids.

- Mental illness and substance abuse disorders resulting from the father's absence can reduce capacities for responsible parenting when boys become dads.

The above statistics clearly show how the direct impacts of absentee fatherhood can be predictably perpetuated from one generation to another. The perpetuation effect may also stem from eroded values, an emotional vacuum, and learned behaviors passed on from generation to generation. When someone experiences abandonment from a father and the resulting wounds and rejection arise from it, they seem to model their lives unconsciously after their wounds, thereby replicating the same results in their children. When the pressure of life comes to fathers who were abandoned in childhood, they are more likely to respond like their fathers, leaving their own children. That vicious cycle and a huge curse must be deliberately broken.

WHAT'S IN A CURSE?

A curse is an inherited adversity founded on ancestral sin and failures. A curse is the opposite of a blessing. The blessing is a supernatural empowerment to succeed in life. A curse, therefore, is a supernatural empowerment to fail. The supernatural force behind a curse causes people's lives to go in a certain negative way. A curse carries a compulsive force that ensures these behaviors are transferred to the next generation. That is why it perpetuates further despite the individual effort to make rational choices. A curse sentences people to calamity, negativity, or misfortune. A cursed man labors uncontrollably under adversity, disappointment, and frustration.

The absentee fathers' curse brings one under uncontrollable compulsive force to abandon one's wife and children. It causes one to come under a spiritual system of restrictions and adversity, predisposing a man to leave his family. The absentee fathers' curse exemplifies a tragic pattern propagating harm and dysfunction across descendant lines.

It is so important to see absentee fatherhood as a curse. Unless we identify the menace of absentee fathers as a generational curse, we will neither reach forth to obtain deliverance from the demonic powers that perpetuate it across generations nor be able to deal with it holistically.

CURSES AND LEGAL GROUNDS

Curses thrive on legal grounds. Until you understand the concept of legal grounds, you will not appreciate how curses arise. A legal ground is built on the law of sowing and reaping. A legal ground is a sin that brings about a curse on an individual, family, or lineage. It is like the carcass that attracts the vultures (Matthew 24:28). The book of Ecclesiastes has this to say:

"He that diggeth a pit shall fall into it; and whoso breaketh a hedge, a serpent shall bite him." (Ecclesiastes 10:8).

That means, without a pit, the serpent will not have access to bite. The pit is technically a breach or an opening that creates access. Sin is the breach; a curse is the serpent.

In the book of Proverbs, the Bible says, "As the bird by wandering, as the swallow by flying, so the curse causeless shall not come... (Proverbs 26:2). In other words, a curse, like a bird, will not land without a cause (landing place), much like an airplane cannot land without a landing place (airport). In other words, the strength of a curse is a legal ground (sin).

GENERATIONAL SINS

Generational sins open the door to curses and demonic spirits who come into play to enforce generational curses. When a curse is successfully in place in an individual, family, or lineage, a supernatural force enforces and perpetuates it across generational lines. When a curse is in place, there is a resulting judgment declared. When Adam and Eve sinned against God in the garden, a curse was proclaimed on the ground for their sake. As a result, life became difficult from that time onwards.

The generational effect of absent fathers' curses is very alarming because it causes children to inherit pain from fathers, who also inherited wounds, brokenness, and pain from their fathers. And more so, by the principle of modeling, the curse further trails down family trees.

When the absentee fathers' curse is in place, sons inherit exile, and daughters inherit rejection—predictable abandonment, spiritual poverty, and shattered identity, which they, in turn, pass from one descendant to the next. Absentee fathers' curse is a huge burden on families, communities, and nations.

And how exciting it is to know that the curse can be broken. A family that has labored under its burden hopes to finally become totally free. Here are a few practical steps for breaking the absentee father's curse:

Step 1: It begins with Awareness

Breaking the cycle of the absentee fathers' curse requires self-awareness, self-mastery, and moral courage across generations. If you want to break free, begin taking quality time to intentionally reflect deeply on your past and present experiences. The purpose of this exercise is to understand the particular fatherhood trauma and wounds you are dealing with. Furthermore, you can also make some inquiries about your family. A family pattern usually sees a generational curse. Knowing the peculiar pattern in your family will provide you a rich clue about what to expect in your life. If you engage in such enquirers, not only will it equip you to break free from such patterns, but it will also put you in a position to make conscious and quality choices and decisions that are geared to truncate such generational curses in your family. Otherwise, you will be controlled by your mere impulses. When you evaluate yourself, you can tell what you will likely face in the future. And by choosing to change your lifestyle based on the insight you now have about yourself, you can completely alter the trajectory of your life.

Step 2: Engage in repentance

As soon as you become aware of the generational patterns in your family lineage, the next thing to do is identificational repentance. Generational curses manifest as a peculiar family pattern that affects everybody who hails from that bloodline. The origin of generational curses is generational sins. The sins in your bloodline are responsible for the curses on your bloodline. However, if these sins are repented of appropriately, it lays the foundation for breaking free from such generational curses. Identificational repentance is repenting on behalf of your ancestors. It involves a personal identification with their shortcomings to receive forgiveness for the generational sin by which they came under satanic bondage and oppression.

By the way, repentance involves a complete change of mind, which results in a shift in behavior and lifestyle. Repentance is more than the feeling of remorse. This step is very vital in obtaining deliverance from generational curses, regardless of how it manifests in the life of an individual or family. If you are already an absent father, the way forward for you will also involve repenting of the sin of abandoning your family. That will also mean acknowledging the harm done, apologizing to children, and resuming presence in their lives. It means paying child support without strings, respecting mothers, and defending children's best interests. It means putting their needs first by constantly sacrificing their personal needs. That is the immediate proof that you have genuinely repented as a runaway father.

As soon as this is done, the legal ground upon which Satan and his demon spirit are standing to perpetuate a generational curse is broken. Remember, curses operate on the grounds of legality. And if those legal grounds are not dealt with, there will be no chance for freedom. If you repent, you have set the groundwork for your deliverance.

Step 3: Obtain deliverance by prayer

The next step is to engage in deliverance prayers. In deliverance prayer, the spirits responsible for perpetuating ancestral behaviors and curses are cast out, and their strongholds over their victims are broken. Jesus has paid the price that guarantees our total liberty; it's up to us to obtain such freedom by consciously engaging in deliverance prayers.

In some cases, persistent emotional bondage or dysfunction may be the result of spiritual strongholds that have taken root in a family over generations. When demonic spirits take over in enforcing negative patterns and sins that sustain such realities, a generational curse is born. Generational curses are often sustained by negative and sinful habits which travel across generations. That is the reason deliverance is required to break such generational patterns.

When a behavior is only natural, it can be broken by simply changing your actions and habits that caused them in the first place. However, if such behaviors result from a generational curse, then behavioral change is insufficient to break free from them; an outright deliverance will be required.

The beautiful thing is that the gospel provides us with many examples of Jesus' ministry of deliverance. Throughout the gospels, we see Jesus practically ejecting unclean spirits and setting the oppressed free through the authority of His name and the power of the Holy Spirit. And like Jesus, the church is called to proclaim deliverance to the captives and freedom to the oppressed (Luke 4:18-19).

Get a Deliverance minister.

However, not all believers are equipped enough to cast out these spirits. Although every believer has been given the authority to cast out demons, not all believers have developed themselves well enough to exercise their God-given authority in Christ. That is why you may need a trained deliverance minister who can come and help pray for your freedom and that of your family members.

Through the gift of discernment plus keen observation, coupled with experience, such ministers can both identify issues like bitterness, rage, fear, addiction, pride, sexual sin, occult history, and other open doors to demonic influences, as well as deal with them. As these legal grounds are removed through repentance and renunciation, deliverance prayer casts out the spirits and breaks spiritual strongholds in Jesus' mighty name.

Step 4: Renew your mind

After you experience supernatural deliverance, it is essential to renew your mind with God's word. Prayer can cast out the daemons that perpetuate the curses and bring down strongholds. Still, if you continue thinking like your absentee fathers (ancestors), you will perpetuate the curse.

After deliverance comes freedom; deliverance is a function of the spirit and the casting out of evil spirits, but freedom is a function of the mind and the replacement of our faulty thinking patterns with new knowledge and new ways of thinking. The principal instrument for mind renewal is the word of the living God (Romans 12:2). Remember, it is the truth that makes free: "And ye shall know the truth, and the truth shall make you free." John 8:32

EMBRACE GOODLY COUNSELING

This is why you need to embrace godly counseling. The scripture says in the multitude of counsel, there is safety. A word fitly spoken can change the very course of somebody's life. The word of God that is spoken to you can penetrate the spiritual realm, thereby affecting your spirit and keeping the works of the flesh under subjection in your life. Without yielding to godly counseling, through the Word of God, the flesh will become more powerful than the spirit. The works of the flesh will manifest in your life, making you bitter, angry, resentful, withdrawn, insecure, inferior, wrathful, unforgiving, and most importantly, bring yourself under the bondage of sinful generational patterns that perpetuate generational curses.

When the Word of God hits you, you will walk in the fruit of the Holy Spirit. So, what would have caused you untold hurt? Will it have no power over you because the fruit of the spirit is manifested in your life? When this happens, you can appreciate your situation and circumstances. When you allow the spirit to take over your life, you will see the mighty hand of God made manifest on your behalf.

WALKING IN WHOLENESS

As you experience inner deliverance and healing, God restores your childlike trust in Him. You are filled with grace and spiritual empowerment to walk in blessing and overcome the sins of past generations. Restored as sons and daughters, you are positioned and empowered to raise godly offspring, propagate faith, love, and healthy relationships for generations to come, and fulfill the promises of God (Psalm 103:17-18).

The church is in a position to break curses stemming from fathers' absence. Through reconciliation, counseling, inner healing, and deliverance ministry, generational wounds can be healed, dysfunctional cycles terminated, and families made whole in Christ Jesus. May you and your family be the new face of a new generation. May you be an example of a genuinely free generation in Jesus' name!

Chapter Seven
STRATEGIES FOR RECONNECTION

Nothing can be more exciting and fulfilling for a father than reconnecting with his children after a long absence. However, that can mean having to go through a series of challenges. Regardless of what initially caused the separation, it must be abundantly clear that rebuilding relationships requires patience, understanding, and concerted effort. It takes real effort to rebuild what has been broken. You cannot rebuild in a day what probably took several years to destroy; you need to give it some time.

To properly reconnect with your children and, sometimes, family, you must learn how to overcome specific barriers that could interfere with your reconnection and how to rebuild trust with your wife and kids. You must master how to access and utilize all resources that enable reconnection and collaborate with your children and wife to make the reconnection possible. The main focus of this chapter is to identify strategic steps that an absentee father can deploy to reconnect with his children successfully.

RECONNECTION IS POSSIBLE

Is reconnecting with your children and family after a long separation possible? You may ask. Of course, it is. Although the pain of being left by a parent makes the possibility of reconnection a sensitive matter emotionally yet, by approaching it openly, honestly, and with professional support, healing, reconnection, and reconciliation can readily be achieved. As long as you are willing and ready to get back with them following the legal framework for reconnection, reconnection will be successful. Depending on what caused the separation, you might even be able to reunite with your wife. However, if it was due to an outright divorce, you should be able to reconnect with your children. You have to be willing to comply with the legal modalities for reconnection. But whatever the case may be, you need to understand that reconnection is possible.

IT IS VITAL

It is critically essential to reconnect back with your family because your family is your power base and your most valuable relationship on earth. At the end of his life, no one ever bothered about not giving enough attention to business, career, or even material possessions. Of course not! It is always about relationships, especially with your wife and kids, which are vital for your earthly fulfillment. No matter how successful you may be materially, if your family is separated or scattered, you are not truly successful. Your children are central to your earthly legacy. If your family is pulled apart, you will never have peace, no matter how successful you are in other areas. Here are other reasons a reconnection is vital:

1. Every child needs a father

Regardless of age, children benefit emotionally, socially, and even academically from having an active and positive paternal influence. Your presence and involvement can provide support, security, guidance, and unconditional love.

2. You need your children

One thing is certain: being separated from your children can negatively impact your own emotional well-being and sense of meaning and purpose. However, when you reconnect with them, you get the opportunity to be their father again. It is only through this opportunity that you begin to nurture and protect them again.

3. Family bonds important

If a family bond is important to you, you will appreciate why reconnecting with your family is a great idea and the best thing to do. There is no stronger bond and support system than what a united family provides.

4. Reinforce identity & self-esteem

Children gain a significant portion of their identity and self-confidence from parental relationships. This provides a foundation that withstands later challenges. Without this, they will remain confused about who they really are. Reconnecting with your children allows you to model true manhood to them, especially to your boys. And for the girls, your modeling helps them appreciate and understand the place of men later in their lives.

FUTURE SUPPORT SYSTEM

Your family is your most incredible support system, now and in the future. What better support system can a person have than the support of his immediate family? Even though total trust may sometimes seem impossible to regain after the painful abandonment, a reconnection opens up possibilities of a new level of friendship and the moral support necessary to face future life challenges.

YOUR PRESENCE ENABLES THEIR DEVELOPMENT

A father's presence in the life of his children supports nearly all aspects of their growth. It provides the kids a solid emotional, cognitive, and social support system. It enables them to grow and develop effectively in every aspect of their lives. Consequently, as a father, you must prioritize your reconnection with them. Only in doing so will you position them to thrive in the real world. Reconnecting with your family will help you repair the broken relationship with them, thereby safeguarding their future from many strange vices.

EMBRACE THE PROCESS

Although the loss of years can never be totally recovered by a reconnection, family members can, at least, have a more positive future to look forward to. The fulfillment that will come from a successful reconciliation far outweighs any bitterness or betrayal lingering from the past abandonment. However, for reconnection to happen, all parties must embrace the process with patience and diligence. No matter how long your family has been separated, you can get back together if you are willing and ready to pay the price.

You must embrace the process with a deep sense of humility. As long as you still care about your ego, offenses, or hurts, you are not ready for a successful reconnection with your loved ones. It starts with you facing whatever huddle may arise along the way. You must be willing to play along to accomplish your ultimate purpose of reconnection and reconciliation. Remember, reconnection holds the key to hope for the future.

BE COMMITTED TO THE PROCESS

You have to understand how deeply the wounds of an absent father and long separation can run. One of the biggest issues is that children who their fathers leave behind grow up with a lot of unanswered questions. The lasting damage that is caused by fathers abandoning their children and family makes it difficult for the reconciliation process. However, as long as the parties involved are committed to the process and willing to do the hard work, then reconciliation is almost guaranteed.

DIFFERENT RESPONSES

It is crucial to understand the dynamics of the reconciliation process and the challenges that may come into play. For instance, if the abandoned children have grown into adulthood before any contact from the absent father is made, their immediate response may be that of anger, confusion, or rejection. And that is understandably so since the children may probably have gotten used to doing life without their father. In other words, a father's sudden re-appearance in their life may seem repulsive rather than exciting.

There is virtually no excuse that can ever make up for the challenges and traumas they have had to go through because their father left home or was separated from them. However, having a chance to directly address what may seem like ages of unanswered questions can be a great time of nurturing and healing. Sometimes, it is even the desire to be acknowledged and loved that forms the motivation for reconciliation.

Every father who makes reconciliation moves usually does so because they feel a sense of guilt and regret for abandoning or whatever may have transpired in the past and sincerely hopes to be forgiven. Every father desires to be urgently reconciled with his children. Imagine the lost time and opportunities a father may have lost living without his children. But that is going to be without resistance.

BE PREPARED FOR INITIAL RESISTANCE

Make no mistakes about it: the beginning part of any reconciliation process can come with a lot of disappointments, considering that old wounds are bound to be reopened by the sudden appearance of someone you have probably long mourned their absence in your life. If someone who has hurt you suddenly shows up, you are compelled to immediately re-live all your hurts. At least before you start considering any reconciliation, you will first feel the pain of your past disappointments. That is the reason people are often advised to get professional counselors involved in the process.

Imagine the once abandoned child has grown into adulthood and now has a family or children. What do you think will happen when the absent father shows up? Indeed, there would be a lot of initial resistance and, in some cases, complications. But as the conversation progresses, both children and grandchildren may begin to feel empathy for their father or now grandfather, leading to vulnerability. Such vulnerable moments create the greatest opportunity for reconnection and later reconciliation.

People will usually show empathy when they understand where you have been and what you have been through. As long as the father puts in sustained effort and respects any roadblocks that his children or wife may put up, a meaningful connection could still form. In other words, when you start, expect initial resistance. You are probably joking if you expect someone you probably abandoned all these long years to open their arms and embrace you immediately. That means you are not being realistic. There is no magic about these things; it will work if you get it right. To get it right, you must follow some guidelines for reconnection and reconciliation. Otherwise, you will find yourself pouring water on rocks.

OVERCOME PERSONAL BARRIERS

Suppose you have separated from your family over a lengthy period, with much hurt but desire to reconnect with them. In that case, you should expect psychological barriers rooted in guilt, shame, and fear of rejection. Of course, you don't expect everything to go smoothly. Do you? And so before you begin to contact them, you must first consider overcoming your inner barriers. Most of the time, what hinders people from taking steps necessary for their progress is not necessarily external factors but internal ones. Internal barriers are more difficult to overcome than external ones. These internal barriers that must be overcome include unresolved trauma, addictions, anger, guilt, unrealistic expectations, fear, rejection, emotional and financial instability, etc. Each of these barriers requires methodical, personalized means of dismantling them, based on the father's specific state of mind depending on the prevalent circumstances of his life. Of course, there are also external barriers to face. However, showing up for your family after such a significant period of separation or even divorce means showing up at your best, ready to overcome every obstacle, regardless of whether they are internal or external.

STRIVE TO REBUILD TRUST

The next most critical step would be to build trust. Before you attempt reconciliation, you must first rebuild trust. Trust is necessary to have reconciliation. Trust is like a glass cup; when it is broken, to rebuilt, it is nearly impossible. Rebuilding trust is the most challenging aspect of reconnecting with your family. And that is the reason you have to be patient with the process. You may give up at the slightest sign of resistance if you are not patient. But if you can work on certain key areas, you can rebuild trust and win the hearts of your loved ones. Here are some of the critical steps you can immediately take to rebuild trust with your once-abandoned loved ones:

1. **Prove your consistency.**

Start by making small promises and keeping them. In other words, if you set a schedule with them, you must endeavor to keep it. It proves consistency and commitment and is a sign that you are willing to turn a new leaf.

2. **Relocate closer to them**

Moving closer to them is a perfect way to show a renewed commitment to your family. You cannot claim you want to be reunited with them and stay far from them. That will sometimes require you to relocate to a place close to them. That way, you can be both present and accessible to them.

3. **Prioritize their events**

Suppose you are the kind of father who was never present at your children's past critical events, especially during separation. In that case, deliberately creating time to be there for their birthdays, ceremonies, and sporting events will go a long way in proving your trust.

4. **Be deliberate about bonding time**

If you want your children and wife to learn to trust you again, then you must become deliberate about bonding with them. Create a quality time of one-on-one bonding where all of you can be together. That could also serve as an opportunity for robust conversations that help your children open up certain challenges to you.

5. Find opportunities for sacrifice

There is no greater way to show renewed commitment than through deliberate sacrifices for your loved ones. You have to find opportunities to be financially involved in their lives. Find out bills that need to be paid and go out of your way to pay them. You can also provide your car for their movements and mentorship, as the case may be. Ultimately, rebuilding trust takes time and patience. If you are consistent and diligent, over time, you will regain the trust of your family.

KNOW YOUR LEGAL RIGHTS AND ACCESS

If you are seriously hoping to reconnect with your children, consider the overall legal implications of your intention. You have to know what the laws say about your rights and access to your children. Depending on some factors, re-establishing contact could be simple or involve specific complex legal processes. Evaluate your situation and options clearly by considering the following:

1. Marital status

If married, reconnecting with children is a private discussion with your spouse. If divorced, the existing custody agreement should dictate how it should be done.

2. Current custody arrangement

Renegotiating access rights might require further litigation if there is no formal legal custody or primary custody was awarded to their mother. And that means you need to understand your rights regarding the law fully.

3. Cohabitation of children

In cases where children live outside the family home with relatives, the father needs to consider the guardianship factors since they define the limits of his access. In other words, additional consent is required.

4. State-specific laws

Laws about child custody and visitation rights of fathers vary from one state to another. It is, therefore, crucial to study your state to know what applies.

5. Termination of rights

In worst-case scenarios, total severance of paternal rights could block contact. If actualized, restarting the relationship could require extensive litigation.

6. Child support obligations

Lack of financial support could complicate progress

reconnecting. That requires that a father endeavor to resolve any outstanding payments. That shows good faith as a father.

7. Third party arbitration

To avoid the expense of lawsuits for access rights, private arbitration using qualified mediators may help negotiate compromises agreeable to all parties.

You can begin the reconnection process once clarity is obtained regarding legal constraints or channels needed to facilitate renewed access. In some cases, depending on what comes up, fathers can directly pursue additional rights via proper avenues. Therefore, it is great to consult family lawyers before reconnection. Once all these legal requirements are in place, a father is on his way to a successful reconnection.

As a father, you must realize that strong, healthy, and united families fulfill your joy and reinforce your sense of purpose and accomplishment. Your desire and attempt to reconnect with your family is a sign that you recognize and acknowledge that family relationships matter beyond any temporary failures you may have experienced in the past. The fact that you failed does not make you a failure. Instead, failure teaches you vital lessons about life. Failure shows you the things that won't work, those that will work, and why. You learn how to make things work better next time from past failures. And while you cannot change history, you can most decidedly change the future. You can create a new future filled with bliss for yourself and your loved ones.

Now that you are ready for a renewed commitment to your loved ones, you must know how to get things back on track. Of course, patience, wisdom, dedication, tremendous courage, and sometimes, many legal hurdles are required to make it happen, but the beauty and joy of finally reuniting with your family far outweigh any sacrifice you may make in the process. In the end, a once-broken family will be reunited again, and the power of God will graciously heal once-wounded hearts. You will see positive results if you are willing to put in the necessary work.

Chapter Eight
A FINAL WORD FOR EVERYONE

Every father has an immense responsibility to love, protect, and provide for his family. Fathers must raise and guide their children in a positive and empowering way. These responsibilities can sometimes feel overwhelming and daunting, with many complex decisions to make that will shape not only the future of your wife and children but also that of society. The role of a father comes with a lot of challenges. Therefore, in such challenging times, godly counsel becomes invaluable. But to benefit from such godly counsel, you must learn to place a high premium on God's wisdom.

There are three kinds of people you cannot help. Firstly, you cannot help anyone who does not believe they have a problem. As long as you are still denying your problems, you cannot be helped. Call it challenges, hard times, or unfavorable situations; they are bound to arise. Challenges are an inevitable part of life. They will come to test your character, capacity, and resolve. And if you are not spiritually and mentally tough, they will distort the peaceful rhythm of your existence. If you cannot acknowledge your problems, you cannot solve them; neither can anyone else help you do so.

The second kind of people you cannot help are those who believe you are their problem. If someone you are trying to help thinks you are responsible for their problems, you cannot help them. The third group of you cannot help but

shock you tremendously. They are those who will never accept godly counsel for their challenges. You cannot help anyone who has no respect for scriptural perspectives on the issues of life. You cannot help someone who has no respect for your wisdom.

GOD'S COUNSEL IS POTENT

There is immeasurable power in Godly counsel. Those who value it will not only be established and prosper in life but will also be guaranteed victory over all life's challenges. Whether you are a father, mother, or child, your value for God's words will decide how well you will respond to all life's challenges. Suppose you find yourself, directly or indirectly, imparted by the trauma of absentee fatherhood.

In that case, whether as the absent father himself, a wounded mother left behind to raise children alone, or the vulnerable children growing up without a dad, this chapter is my final word of counsel, wisdom, and encouragement to you.

The Bible says, "Where no counsel is, the people fall: but in the multitude of counselors there is safety." (Proverbs 11:14). Your safety is in the counsel you choose to receive and live by. Amazingly, no better counselor exists than our Heavenly Father Himself, who operates in us through the Holy Spirit and His word. And God's word is His wisdom (Deuteronomy 4:6). As you embrace the counsel that I now present, especially as it concerns you, you will experience a huge transformation both in your response to adversity and in every area of your life.

A WORD FOR FATHERS

As a father, realize you have a huge responsibility to your wife, children, and community. You may not presently be in your children's or their mother's life, yet it's up to you to cater for them. It is your job to nurture them in the way of God. A well-raised child will pattern himself after the authority and lifestyle modeled by his father. And that is how you can duplicate yourself.

It is your job to lay a solid foundation of principles, dignity, morals, good character, reputation, and hard work. You must work hard to create wealth and leave a reasonable inheritance for your children. The scripture admonishes every father to do so (Proverbs 13:22). That way, your children will forever be proud of you.

LAY A SOLID FOUNDATION FOR THEM

The foundation of a great father comes from God. God is the one who establishes a good foundation upon which you can build. If you build upon that foundation of the word, you will have order in your home and a loving and flourishing family. If you build your house upon God and everything that God is, you will receive the same for yourself and your household. If you successfully plant the word of God into their virgin souls, it stays with them all through their lives so that when challenges show up later in their lives, they can withstand them.

However, if something goes wrong, and you have to leave home as a father, do not let things get out of hand by totally abandoning your wife and children. How you act can affect your children's future negatively or positively. Remember, your wife is your companion and God's favorite gift to you, and you cannot treat her however you want. If you have left your family or been separated from them for whatever reason, you must endeavor not to abandon your children physically or emotionally. Even if you cannot be there physically for them, do not abandon them emotionally. Do everything within your power to remain active and relevant in their lives. And that requires you to call them often, connect with them, and be physically present when possible.

Whether or not you are in tune with their mother, you must embrace them fully as your children and take good care of them. We have seen how destructive it is to disappear from your children's lives completely. You cannot let that happen to your children. Regardless of how bad the relationship between you and the mother of your children is, it would help if you found ways to bridge the communication gap for the sake of your children.

Ensure you provide for their needs. It is your duty as a father to provide for your children's emotional, physical, and financial needs. But more than merely providing for their several needs, meet their spiritual needs also. In other words, cover your children firmly in prayer. Pray for their protection, provision, emotional healing, and supernatural strength that can only come from above. Though you may not be able to hold them in your arms every time, you can always lift them into the everlasting arms of their Heavenly Father, who promises to be a Father to the fatherless.

Seek counseling if you have to; make sure you are taking steps in the best interest of your children and not just seeking to satiate your ego. Understand that your children's future is paramount and requires the highest commitment possible. Use every opportunity available to impart them with wisdom and connect with them at the necessary levels.

If you make a quality decision backed with a commitment to give your children the best of you, loving, protecting, and providing for them, you will break the cycle and generational curse of the absent father in your life. It doesn't matter what has happened to your family in the past; if you still want to be a loving, caring, and responsible father, it's possible. You can change the trajectory of your children and family by simply accepting responsibility.

A WORD FOR MOTHERS

As a mother, you owe it to your children to build a home filled with love, joy, respect, and honor. You must labor to create peace in your home. Nothing is more important to a man than peace. Without peace in the home, the family cannot thrive. The worst thing a woman can do is to create a hostile environment in her home, either by constantly disagreeing with her husband, nagging, or being generally disrespectful to him. When a woman becomes disrespectful to her husband, or if she constantly nags, she creates a hostile environment for her man, thereby driving him away from the home. But if you choose to get things right, you will have a loving and fulfilling home.

Unfortunately, things don't always work nearly as successfully as expected. Life does happen to people sometimes. And when it does, you must know what to do. If your husband or father of your children chooses to vanish, leaving you with the huge burden of catering for the children, as a solo parent, stay strong. Do not let the burden of loving, providing, and nurturing the children alone crush you completely. When a woman is in that state, you can only imagine the level of emotional, physical, and financial burden she is carrying alone.

As a mother experiencing these conditions, I want you to know that though the challenges before you may seem staggering, the injustices infuriating, and the fears paralyzingly, there is a way out in God. You must learn to cast all your cares on God, who loves and cares for you far beyond how any man can ever care for you. You might even struggle with unforgiveness, bitterness, and the thought of doing something crazy. Yet none of those reactions can serve your children's best interest or your own. As terribly tricky as your situation may be, responding thoughtfully and strategically offers the only real hope for you to emerge stronger and victorious.

When a father leaves, the mother must be open to their kids. In other words, sit down and explain exactly what is happening between you and their father to the children. Let them know why the relationship did not continue and what has happened to cause the absence of their father from the home. It doesn't matter how sour or bitter the relationship was with your partner; tell them the truth. Otherwise, you will lose their trust.

No matter what, never curse their father in their presence. Sometimes, mothers play a dangerous role by planting the wrong seeds in the minds and hearts of their children.

Don't do that. Do not be the kind of mother who will help your children to form a negative mental picture of their dad. Instead, allow the children to have a good relationship with their father by sharing only his positive side. When you distort a father's image before the children, you instigate rebellion in their hearts. As a result, you will cause them to rebel from your authority and every other form of authority. That is why we have so many criminals in society today. They have carried their rebellion outside. The seed of evil sown in their life by their mother causes the children to become evil. And in the future, such children become angry fathers and mothers who will probably perpetuate absent fatherhood.

COUNSEL FOR THE FATHERLESS CHILD

If you have been left by your father, for whatever reason, realize that it is not your fault. You are not responsible for your father's absence in your life or whatever transpired between your father and mother. Moreover, all that is in the past now, and you must refuse to allow guilt to torment your life.

Do not be bitter towards your absent father or angry and rebellious against your mother like I was. Instead, continue to rejoice in his grace. And in due time, God will search with His angels and cause your father to return to you as long as he is still alive. And if God grants you the grace to see your absent father again, give him the gift of your love.

One of the greatest gift you can give your father is to love him unconditionally. Of course, you may have been hurt and wounded by his actions. But seeing him again allows you to forgive and reconcile with him, knowing he could have acted in ignorance.

When the need arises, reach out to a counselor and seek godly mentors with the heart and experience to see you through the process. Above all, lean on the loving arm of your Heavenly Father. Cultivate an intimate relationship with Him. When loneliness, anger, or shame closes on you, learn to pour out your heart like a drink offering to your father in heaven through prayer, praise, and worship. When you do, His mighty arm will touch and heal you where it hurts the most. He will heal your every hurt and answer every question you secretly grapple with.

The wounds resulting from a father's absence can be devastating, with the potential to emotionally devastate children for decades. Yet out of such anguish, God as Redeemer and restorer can bring wholeness and wisdom to all impacted negatively. Fathers must maintain a connection with their kids at all costs and seek common grounds for reconciliation with both kids and mothers. Mothers must fight to uphold stability while releasing bitterness and disappointment. Children must seek to encounter God intimately as the perfect father from whom they can find their identity rather than focus on the loss of their earthly father.

The most beautiful part is that when all parties look to Christ for healing from their hurt and brokenness, beauty suddenly emerges from the ashes of their loss, and negativity gradually disappears. The absence of a father is not the end of life; it only creates an opportunity for a new flavor to life's journey. And as challenging as it may seem, God has your back. He will always work it for your good. Hallelujah!

REFERENCES

Chapter 1

U.S. Census Bureau. (2023). Living arrangements of children under 18 years old: 1960 to present. Washington, D.C.: U.S. Census Bureau.

U.S. Census Bureau, National Single Parent Day.

https://www.census.gov/newsroom/stories/single-parent-day.html

https://www.ncbi.nlm.nih.gov/pmc/articles/PMC2636517/

Chapter 2

https://www.fatherhood.org/father-absence-statistic

Chapter 4

https://divorce.com/blog/divorce-statistics/#:~:text=The%20divorce%20rate%20regarding%20second,once%20compared%20to%20all%20adults.

https://www.statista.com/statistics/276025/us-percentage-of-births-to-unmarried-women/

https://adoptioncouncil.org/publications/single-parent-adoption-the-process-and-experience-of-adopting-unpartnered/

Chapter 6

https://ifstudies.org/blog/life-without-father-less-college-less-work-and-more-prison-for-young-men-growing-up-without-their-biological-father

https://www.all4kids.org/news/blog/a-fathers-impact-on-child-development/

About the Book

Fathers play a pivotal role in the upbringing and development of their children. As fathers, they are responsible for loving, protecting, and providing for their children and raising, guiding, and positively influencing them. Unfortunately, many fathers leave their wives and children, exposing them to many traumatic experiences. In this exciting new book, the author reveals why so many fathers leave, the struggles and trauma that affected family members have to go through, how to heal the wounds of an absent father and strategies for reconnection. Whether as a father, single mother, or an abandoned child, the insight shared in this book will completely transform your life!

www.ingramcontent.com/pod-product-compliance
Lightning Source LLC
LaVergne TN
LVHW051843080426
835512LV00018B/3040